F. Scott Fitzgerald

and the American Dream

D0815947

813
F5537
F157f

F. Scott Fitzgerald

and the American Dream

By William A. Fahey

Thomas Y. Crowell Company New York

The quotations in the book are from *Babylon Revisited and Other Stories,
The Stories of F. Scott Fitzgerald, Taps at Reveille, This Side of Paradise,
The Beautiful and Damned, The Great Gatsby, Tender Is the Night,*
and *The Last Tycoon,* all by F. Scott Fitzgerald and published by Charles
Scribner's Sons. Other quotations are from *Afternoon of an Author* by
F. Scott Fitzgerald, published by the Bodley Head; *The Letters of F. Scott
Fitzgerald,* edited by Andrew Turnbull and published by Bantam; *The Far
Side of Paradise* by Arthur Mizener, published by Houghton Mifflin Com-
pany; and *The Crack-Up* by F. Scott Fitzgerald, edited by Edmund Wil-
son and published by New Directions. The lines of verse by Wallace
Stevens are from "The Snow Man," *The Collected Poems of Wallace
Stevens,* published by Alfred A. Knopf; those by Robert Frost are from
"Provide, Provide," *The Complete Poems of Robert Frost,* published by
Henry Holt and Company; those by T. S. Eliot are from "The Waste
Land," *The Complete Poems and Plays, 1909–1950,* published by Har-
court, Brace and Company.

Copyright © 1973 by William A. Fahey

All rights reserved. Except for use in a review,
the reproduction or utilization of this work in
any form or by any electronic, mechanical, or
other means, now known or hereafter invented,
including xerography, photocopying, and record-
ing, and in any information storage and retrieval
system is forbidden without the written permission
of the publisher. Published simultaneously in
Canada by Fitzhenry & Whiteside Limited, Toronto.

Designed by Angela Foote

Manufactured in the United States of America
ISBN 0–690–00078–2

LIBRARY OF CONGRESS CATALOGING IN PUBLICATION DATA

Fahey, William A
  F. Scott Fitzgerald and the American dream.

  (Twentieth-century American writers)
  Bibliography: p.
  1. Fitzgerald, Francis Scott Key, 1896–1940.
I. Title.
PS3511.19Z616   813'.5'2   73–4523
ISBN 0–690–00078–2

1 2 3 4 5 6 7 8 9 10

49459

For My Mother and Father

Contents

F. Scott Fitzgerald

and the American Dream

1

Two Families

In the cellar of forgotten memories comprising what F. Scott Fitzgerald calls "all the complicated dark mixture of my youth and infancy that made me a fiction writer instead of a fireman or a soldier" is a grave, the "too recent mound of dirt in the corner," as he describes it in "Author's House," a metaphoric biographical sketch published in *Esquire* magazine in 1936. "That," he says in the sketch, "is where I buried my first childish love of myself, my belief that I wasn't the son of my parents but a son of a king, a king who ruled the world."

The myth of the two families, the royal and the humble, is of course a familiar one. The fundamental source of the myth is in what Freud describes as the "family romance" of the child, who early in life overestimates the stature and significance of his parents, representing them in dreams as kings and queens, and later, under the stress of rivalry and the strains of daily living, develops a critical

1

attitude toward them. As seen by the psychoanalyst, the two families of the myth—the royal and the humble—are thus revealed as two aspects of his own family as they appear to the child in successive periods of his life.

The interesting thing about Fitzgerald's version of the myth is that having announced his noble heritage at age nine, when he told neighbors that he had been found on the doorstep tagged with the royal name of Stuart, the "too recent mound of dirt" in "Author's House" indicates that he was close to forty before he buried the myth in the cellar of forgotten memories. That means that the mythic machinery of parental demotion was kept in service for a long time. Moreover, Fitzgerald sees the symbolic interment as "the burial of my first childhood love of myself," suggesting, perhaps, that narcissism lay behind the adoption of the myth, rather than a maturing insight into the limitations of his parents. Indeed he tells his daughter Scottie in one of his letters to her: "I didn't know till 15 that there was anyone in the world except me, and it cost me *plenty*."

Since Scottie Fitzgerald was approaching fifteen at the time her father wrote, perhaps the age mentioned was more convenient for fatherly moralizing than accurate in the chronology of self-description. In any case, fifteen would have been but the beginning of the process of discovery that the world was not made in his own image, a process that was to take years and to cost so much. In fact, Arthur Mizener, Fitzgerald's biographer, says that Fitzgerald "never buried his past because he was too naive to realize that you are supposed to believe it is dead." Until the time of the terrible "Crack-Up," in 1936, when his world fell apart, Fitzgerald continued, with at least one part of his mind, to believe that he was the son of a king who ruled the world and that he would never die like other people. The belief was part of his strength as a writer, for in the rich fantasy life of this "once and future king" the past continued to inform the present. In a sense, of course, it always does. But it did so for Fitzgerald with such vivid intensity that the past he recalled in his writing had all the immediacy of the present. The cost of the fantasy was indeed high. It was to include, among other things, his wife's sanity, and with the intrusion into his life of a different destiny from the one he imagined so intensely for himself, the fragmentation of his own career as a writer.

That career began, according to Fitzgerald, three months before he was born, on September 24, 1896, in St. Paul, Minnesota, when his mother lost her first two children. Speculating later on his artistic genesis, Fitzgerald returns to that event—". . . I think I started then to be a writer."

Clearly Molly McQuillan Fitzgerald's loss had important consequences for her son. Coddled, pampered, and indulged, he learned early to expect attention; indeed, to require it. He was constantly being put forward before family groups and friends to sing popular songs, to recite verse that he had memorized, to perform. Preferred by his mother, he began to prefer himself; shown off, he became a show-off. Predictably he was rejected by boys and girls his own age. His recollections of his childhood and youth are filled with episodes of disappointment and humiliation—the birthday party to which nobody came, the summer camp where he was "desperately unpopular," the schoolboy gang into which he "just didn't fit," the St. Paul's Academy magazine in which he was sarcastically depicted as the boy who knew "how to run the School" and where someone with adolescent brutality queried, "Will someone poison Scotty or find some means to shut his mouth?"

But his mouth couldn't be shut. Denied social acceptance, he turned to amateur theatricals in a neighbor's attic, where casting himself as a romantic hero with a red sash and a pasteboard sword, he could triumph vicariously. Or he would turn his disasters into victories in the stories that he industriously scribbled throughout his boyhood, skipping homework to write late into the night and continuing his efforts behind a book in class the next day, until his scholastic record was a shambles at St. Paul's Academy, the private country day school he attended. By the age of thirteen he regarded himself as an "inveterate author." Later, looking back on his boyhood from the perspective of middle age, he couldn't recall a time when he had not wanted to write more than he had wanted to do anything else.

Strangely enough, Fitzgerald's mother, who indulged him in everything else and spoiled him terribly, failed to encourage his writing. In fact, she discouraged it, having little literary taste herself—one of Fitzgerald's biographers describes her as an omnivorous reader of bad books, on the level of the lady poetasters Alice and Phoebe Cary—and being eager, anyway, to see her son follow the pattern of his grandfather McQuillan, who had made a fortune in the wholesale grocery business, starting from small beginnings, before he died at the early age of forty-three. Mrs. Fitzgerald was perhaps doubly anxious to have her son follow in the footsteps of her father. First of all, her father had risen from what his grandson would later describe as "straight 1850 potato famine Irish," through energy, industry, and a convenient marriage with the boss's daughter, to a position of affluence with a house on prestigious Summit Avenue, one of "the best streets" in St. Paul. And secondly, her own husband, whom she dominated completely, failed in business, drank heavily, and after brief sojourns in Buffalo and Syracuse, settled in St. Paul as a kind of satellite of the McQuillan family, finding financial security only after the death of Molly's mother, who left her a sizeable inheritance.

The conflict between the affluent McQuillans, who rose from rags to riches, or from potato-famine immigrants to lace-curtain Irish, in a generation, and Fitzgerald's father's family, comprising Scotts and Keys going back to colonial times, where they figured significantly in Maryland history, was an important element in the formation of Fitzgerald's character. Commenting on his background, in a letter written to John O'Hara in 1933, Fitzgerald says:

> I am half black Irish and half old American stock with the usual exaggerated ancestral pretensions. The black Irish half of the family had the money and looked down upon the Maryland side of the family who had, and really had, that certain series of reticences and obligations that go under the poor old battered word "breeding" (modern form "inhibitions.") So being born in that atmosphere of crack, wisecrack and counter-crack I developed a two-cylinder inferiority complex. So if I were elected King of Scotland tomorrow after graduation from Eton, Magdalene to Guards, with an embryonic history which tied me to the Plantagenets, I would still be a parvenu. I spent my youth in alternately crawling in front of the kitchen maids and insulting the great.

The two families have thus a historic dimension as well as a mythic one. Ironically, it is the humble family, or branch, that wields the power, the regal, or aristocratic Maryland branch, dating back to Colonial legislators and including the composer of "The Star-Spangled Banner," for whom Fitzgerald was named, that is subservient. Moreover, the two-family alternative, the humble and the royal, is, so to speak, paradigmatically illustrated in Fitzgerald's parents: his energetic, domineering mother, of whom he was frequently ashamed, and his cultivated but ineffectual father, whom he revered. And, of course, the split appears in Fitzgerald himself, a romantic egoist of astounding proportions with a two-cylinder inferiority complex.

The " 'breeding' (modern form 'inhibitions')" that Fitzgerald "really had," he had from his father, though the parenthetic qualification and the need for emphatic insistence—"really had"—reflect an insecurity based on his mother's more or less constant reminders of Edward Fitzgerald's dependent position in relation to the McQuillans. "Breeding" meant living according to the chivalric code of the old South, imbued in the boy by his father's precept and example. It involved a high sense of personal honor, obligations unobtrusively assumed, and good manners followed almost instinctively. Speaking of his father, Fitzgerald says, "He was much too sure of what he was . . . to doubt for a moment that his own instincts were good."

That was the ideal. But in young Fitzgerald the doubt was present. It took root perhaps on the terrible day in Buffalo in 1908 when he learned that his father had been fired from his job as salesman with Procter and Gamble, and he ran into the house to pray that they wouldn't have to go to the poorhouse. The specter of that event was to haunt Fitzgerald, as the specter of the blacking warehouse haunted Charles Dickens, for the remainder of his life. Recalling the day, Fitzgerald wrote, "That morning he had gone out a comparatively young man, a man full of strength, full of confidence. He came home that evening an old man, a completely broken man. He had lost his essential drive, his immaculateness of purpose. He was a failure the rest of his days."

Remembering his father's failure and fearing it, Fitzgerald strove for success with the energy and determination of the McQuillans. And he strove for their goals—wealth, power, social recognition. But the goals were not enough. They had to be achieved with that immaculateness of purpose that the father, in losing, transmitted to the son.

Of course, Edward Fitzgerald was not the sole transmitter of such fine-spun ideals, nor did he transmit them alone. Unlike the boy's mother, his father encouraged his efforts at writing and nourished them with family legends and tales of the Civil War, readings from the Romantic poets and a recommended literary diet rich in novelists like Sir Walter Scott. In addition there were the boys' books, heavily freighted with elaborate conventions of prep-school behavior and peopled with idealized young men, generally of rather priggish nature, who accomplished wonders on the athletic field or in feats of adventure and deeds of derring-do. These Fitzgerald discovered by himself and imitated assiduously.

Then there was the fact that Fitzgerald was brought up as a Roman Catholic, something of an anomaly in early twentieth-century middle America, where the business ethic and Protestant morality were, if not hand and glove then perhaps matching arms of what has come to be called the Establishment. At age fifteen, Fitzgerald was sent East to the Newman School, a Catholic preparatory school in Hackensack, New Jersey, to recover, through purportedly tough clerical discipline, academic ground lost at St. Paul's. There he came under the influence of Father (later Monsignor) Fay. Cultivated, aristocratic, worldly, a convert to Catholicism who yet retained the manners and bearing of a dandy and something of the detachment and aloofness of the aesthete, Fay cultivated the boy, encouraged his literary ambitions, and won his affection. Later, speaking of the influence of the church on his development, Fitzgerald was to say of Monsignor Fay that he made of the church "a dazzling golden thing dispelling its oppressive mugginess and giving the succession of days upon gray days, passing under its plaintive ritual, the romantic glamour of an adolescent dream."

The appraisal is a just one. And even after Fitzgerald abandoned the church, which he was soon to do, he would take along the peculiar romantic coloring with which Monsignor Fay managed to infuse the Roman Catholic faith. This transference is well illustrated in a story Fitzgerald wrote called "Absolution," published in the *American Mercury* in 1924 and later collected in *All the Sad Young Men.*

The story has been much praised. Too much praised, I think, for it is a derivative story, taking its stereotyped properties from Sherwood Anderson's *Winesburg, Ohio.* These include an unconvincing old loony—Father Schwartz, the parish priest—outfitted with a conventional budget of repressed lusts and a faded carpet, who dreams of a world where "things go glimmering"—believe it or not—and who passes out in a schoolgirl's vision of a carnival, an unconvincingly imagined world of beauty so keenly felt by the poor old priest that he can't take it. There is also a sensitive young boy who escapes harsh reality by periodically chanting the name of his imaginary alter ego—Blatchford Sarnemington! There is, of course, a brutal father and, briefly, a withered ineffectual mother. Inevitably the theme of the story is a contrast between unfeeling repression, imaged in the old priest's stuffy room, and "hot fertile life," imaged variously and about as effectively as the foregoing phrase deserves. The phrase is, by the way, not uncharacteristic of the diction of the piece. When the old priest collapses under the flimsy weight of his vision, his babble peoples the room with voices and faces "until it was crowded with echolalia." And when the boy escapes into the sexy night, a "blue sirocco trembled over the wheat." In Ludwig, S. Dakota!

Despite its limitations, however, "Absolution" has considerable interest for the student of Fitzgerald. The boy in the story, for one thing, is obviously patterned on Fitzgerald himself and reflects, however inadequately, a number of the author's preoccupations. There is, for example, a brief treatment of Fitzgerald's mythic conception of his origins. At confession, with Father Schwartz, the boy lists his minor faults, then pauses. This dialogue follows:

> "Go on, my child."
> "Of—of not believing I was the son of my parents."
> "What?" The interrogation was distinctly startled.
> "Of not believing that I was the son of my parents."
> "Why not?"
> "Oh, just pride," answered the penitent airily.
> "You mean you thought you were too good to be the son of your parents?"
> "Yes, Father." On a less jubilant note.
> "Go on."

When the boy answers "airily," his answer is obviously ironically conceived by Fitzgerald, whose own victory over pride cost him, as he told his daughter, "plenty." Fitzgerald's attitude toward Father Schwartz is less clear. His sober rephrasing of the boy's casual reply appears to unsettle the boy, who responds "on a less jubilant note." But the priest's mechanical "Go on" suggests a failure to count the cost of pride.

Of course, Father Schwartz is to be the chief agent of the reversal ironically suggested by the title of the story. Absolution is not something granted by the church but something taken by the boy as he abandons the restrictive psychology of his father for the freedom and joy of the sensual world.

The boy, who is named Rudolph, has lied in the confessional. Returning to repent his sin, he is reoriented by the disturbed priest:

> All this talking seemed particularly strange and awful to Rudolph, because this man was a priest. He sat there, half terrified, his beautiful eyes open wide and staring at Father Schwartz. But underneath his terror he felt that his own inner convictions were confirmed. There was something ineffably gorgeous somewhere that had nothing to do with God. He no longer thought that God was angry at him about the original lies, because He must have understood that Rudolph had done it to make things finer in the confessional, brightening up the dinginess of his admissions by saying a thing radiant and proud. At the moment when he had affirmed immaculate honor a silver pennon had flapped out into the breeze somewhere and there had been the crunch of leather and the shine of silver spurs and a troop of horsemen waiting for dawn on a low green hill. The sun had made stars of light on their breastplates like the picture at home of the German cuirassiers at Sedan.

Thus Rudolph is reborn, in the glittering light glancing off tin soldiers, as Fitzgerald in tawdry rhetoric transfers from the clerical to the secular world "the romantic glamour of an adolescent dream." Fitzgerald seems to be saying that Rudolph's lie is justified by the imaginative transformation of his surroundings it makes possible. But the language used by the author to indicate the transformation is cheap and pretentious, a kind of lie itself, and it fails of its desired effect.

Adolescence is not always so cheaply conceived in Fitzgerald. As a matter of fact, his prolonged preoccupation with his own boyhood and adolescence, his inability to bury his past, enabled him generally to present those periods with convincing freshness. His egotism kept alive even minor episodes of his life with much of their first blush preserved, and while it made him seem "bossy" or "fresh" to his young contemporaries, whose activities he tried to dominate, that same egotism permitted him to usurp their roles in his fiction and to relive their experiences as reconceived by his own imagination.

There is, of course, a quality of naiveté in all this, but it is a genuine naiveté and the results are very often happy, as in the Basil and Josephine stories, published in *The Saturday Evening Post* between 1928 and 1930. Fitzgerald recognized the essential simplicity, the lack of imaginative reconception of events in these stories, when he resisted the efforts of Maxwell Perkins, his editor at Scribner's, to get him to publish the Basil stories in book form. (Ultimately five of the Basil stories and three of the Josephine stories did go into *Taps at Reveille*, but Perkins had wanted to publish the Basil stories in a separate book by themselves.) Commenting in his notebooks on the resemblance, in circumstances of creation and in conception, between these stories and the Penrod stories of Booth Tarkington, another Princetonian and a man who for a time had been an alcoholic, Fitzgerald expressed the fear that his own drinking bouts might leave him devitalized, as he felt Tarkington had been when he wrote the Penrod stories. The result might have been thin, superficial stories, their characters mere stereotypes of boyhood. The only value of the stories might thus have been an accuracy of detail similar to Tarkington's. He'd have the games right and the childish prattle, the clothes and the gestures, but the stories would have lacked substance.

So Fitzgerald feared. However, for all their lack of depth, the stories in question are neither devitalized nor stereotyped, for they are in fact based on really acute observation. Hence the Basil and Josephine stories manage to capture a good deal of the flavor of life, of the feeling of what it was like to be a boy in love for the first time or a girl bent on subduing the male world, in the early decades of the twentieth century in America.

To be sure, some of the episodes in the stories reflect universal experiences, American only by virtue of place name. Thus in "A Night at the Fair," the young hero, who is the counterpart of F. Scott Fitzgerald, is said to have been responsible for this "cosmic inscription in his last year's Ancient History":

> Basil Duke Lee
> Holly Avenue
> St. Paul
> Minnesota
> United States
> North America
> Western Hemisphere
> The World
> The Universe

Change but a few proper nouns, and it might be from James Joyce's *A Portrait of the Artist as a Young Man*:

> Stephen Dedalus

Class of Elements
Clongowes Wood College
Sallins
County Kildare
Ireland
Europe
The World
The Universe

However, the state fair from which the story "A Night at the Fair" takes its title is, with its "immense exhibits of grain, livestock and farming machinery," its "tumultuous midway," its "whining . . . hoochie-coochie show," its "stuffy tent" called "the Temple of Wheat," and its "grand exhibition of fireworks, culminating in a representation of the Battle of Gettysburg," unmistakably Midwestern America.

Unmistakable, too, is the whole atmosphere of middle-class America evoked in story after story. There is, for example, the Whartons' backyard in "The Scandal Detectives." Though the Whartons' children "had long grown up, their yard was still one of those predestined places where young people gather in the afternoon." It was

> large, open to other yards on both sides, and it could be entered upon skates or bicycles from the street. It contained an old seesaw, a swing and a pair of flying rings; but it had been a rendezvous before these were put up, for it had a child's quality . . . . there were deep shadows there all day long and ever something vague in bloom, and patient dogs around, and brown spots worn bare by countless circling wheels and dragging feet.

There at five o'clock of a summer afternoon

> a small crowd gathered . . . . Basil and Riply rode

their bicycles around abstractedly, in and out of trees, resting now and then with a hand on someone's shoulder, shading their eyes from the glow of the late sun . . . .

Hubert took off his skates, rolled one down his arm and caught it by the strap before it reached the pavement; he snatched the ribbon from Imogene's hair and made off with it, dodging from under her arms as she pursued him, laughing and fascinated, around the yard. He cocked one foot behind the other and pretended to lean an elbow against a tree, missed the tree on purpose and gracefully saved himself from falling. The boys watched him noncommittally at first. Then they, too, broke out into activity, doing stunts and tricks as fast as they could think of them until those on the porch craned their necks at the sudden surge of activity . . . .

Characteristic prejudices appear. Below the bluff, two hundred feet from the Wharton yard, "in sordid poverty," live "the micks—they had merely inherited the name, for they were now largely of Scandinavian descent." When Hubert reports on the ambush staged by "the Scandal Detectives," he fabricates a "gang of toughs," depicting them as "sort of foreignors or something." His father, George P. Blair, interrupts his account of the attack to specify: "Hubert says he thinks they were Italians." Naturally, the "chickens" the boys pick up in "A Night at the Fair" are lower-class girls who go to public schools, have brothers who are fireworks attendants, and, more likely than not, "a bad complexion brooding behind a mask of cheap pink powder." When teamed up with boys from "respectable families," they constitute a grotesque procession:

Along the now empty and brightly illuminated

race track came a short but monstrous procession,
a sort of Lilliputian burlesque of the wild gay life.
At its head marched Hubert Blair and Olive, Hubert prancing and twirling his cane like a drum
major to the accompaniment of her appreciative
screams of laughter. Next followed Elwood Leaming and his young lady, leaning so close together
that they walked with difficulty, apparently
wrapped in each other's arms. And bringing up
the rear without glory were Riply Buckner and
Basil's late companion, rivalling Olive in exhibi-
tionist sound.

As a matter of fact, degrees of a certain kind of sensitivity or cultivation are registered through the boy's relationships with these girls. Hubert Blair, "who possessed the
exact tone that all girls of fourteen, and a somewhat cruder
type of grown women, found irresistible," leads the procession with unself-conscious gusto, though even he has
used a false name to date Olive. Elwood Leaming—"the
dissipated one among the nice boys of the town—he had
drunk beer, he had learned from chauffeurs, he was already
thin from too many cigarettes"—is completely oblivious
to the fact that he is making a spectacle of himself. Riply
Buckner, on the other hand, is close to the sensitive Basil,
who has escaped from the procession altogether and sits in
a box with Gladys Van Schellinger, inhabitant of "the
city's second largest mansion." And the expression on Riply's face is "curiously mixed. At moments he would join in
the general tone of the parade with silly guffaw, at others a
pained expression would flit across his face, as if he doubted
that after all, the evening was a success."

The evening is a success—if not an unqualified one—
for Basil. He has picked up a girl—and managed to evade
her when he discovers her to be "a fright," imposing her on

his sometimes critical friend Riply. He has won the appro-
bation of the high and mighty of St. Paul and sits in their
seats of judgment—on poor Riply. He has even managed
to preserve his own sense of virtue in all this, interceding for
Riply impulsively—and ineffectually—when Riply is criticized by the Van Schellingers for his involvement in the
evening's events. What qualifies his success is Fitzgerald's
marvelously ironic conclusion. For it transpires that Gladys
Van Schellinger, for all her "fresh delicate face," careful
upbringing, and great wealth, shares the tastes of "all girls
of fourteen and a somewhat cruder type of grown women."
After spending the evening watching the fireworks display
with triumphantly virtuous Basil, she invites him to visit
her next day—on condition that he "bring that Hubert
Blair."

Most of the Basil stories are less complexly ironic than
"A Night at the Fair." Both "The Freshest Boy" and "He
Thinks He's Wonderful," for example, turn on a reversal of
sorts. But in neither does the reversal result in the kind of
revaluation of values that the ironic conclusion of "A Night
at the Fair" suggests. Actually "The Freshest Boy," which
is based on Fitzgerald's first horrible year at the Newman
School (St. Regis in the Basil stories), ends with a commitment on the part of Basil to the very regimen of nar-
rowness and stupidity that had made his life a misery at
the school. Spurned and jeered at by his schoolmates, he
has been terribly unhappy at St. Regis. Then, out of the
blue, his mother offers to take him to Europe with her on
a tour she is about to make. But he turns her down. Basil
rationalizes his decision in the following way:

> He could not forgo the moulding of his own des-
> tiny just to alleviate a few months of pain. The
> conquest of the successive worlds of school, college

and New York—why, that was his true dream that
he had carried from boyhood into adolescence,
and because of the jeers of a few boys he had been
about to abandon it and run ignominiously up a
back alley! He shivered violently, like a dog coming out of the water . . . .

But Basil's true dream of conquering successive worlds by
constant application and ending on the pinnacle of success
in New York is only a dream. An awkwardly intrusive episode in the story, involving Ted Fay, a Yale athlete, and
his girl Jerry, a Broadway ingenue, indicates how remote
the dream is from reality. The way to success in New York
for Jerry is through sleeping with Beltzman, a theatrical
producer. And if Ted goes back to Yale, as Basil will to St.
Regis, to belt out home runs with the bases loaded because
he is an ideal to young boys, the effort brings his own
dream of true love no closer to realization. When he says
to Jerry, "Tell him [Beltzman] the truth—that you love
me. Ask him to let you off," she replies, "This isn't musical
comedy, Ted."

In what Arthur Mizener describes in his biography of
Fitzgerald as "a remarkably honest account of himself,"
Fitzgerald reflects on his divided nature:

Psychologically . . . I was by no means the "Captain of my fate" [he recalls]. . . . I was liable to be
swept off my poise into a timid stupidity. I knew
I was "fresh" and not popular with older boys. . . .
Generally—I knew that at bottom I lacked essentials. At the last crisis, I knew I had no real courage, perseverance or self respect.

Basil, making the hard decision and returning to St. Regis
rather than abandoning the struggle and running "ignominiously up a back alley" to Europe with his mother, would

seem to represent Fitzgerald's conception of being captain of one's fate, or in Basil's words, "moulding his own destiny." In this he resembles Ted Fay going back to Yale to belt out home runs with a broken heart. The rhetoric and the melodrama go hand in hand. But since Ted's girl goes to Beltzman and Basil returns to snobbish, venal, conformist schoolmates under the direction of brutal drunkards and cynical incompetents, one wonders if the game is worth the candle. To assume that it is, under the circumstances, is perhaps the surest indication that one lacks "the essentials."

In "He Thinks He's Wonderful" Basil reveals, in the domestic milieu of a St. Paul summer, the same egotism that had resulted in so much frustration when he went East to school. There are a number of reversals in the story, beginning with the one that establishes his popularity with the hometown girls after a year in virtual isolation at St. Regis. However, his self-concern produces, inevitably, a revulsion, and he is ignored on the back seats of automobiles, left out of parties, and so forth. Yet another reversal throws him into the arms of charming Minnie Bibble, who has turned hearts, precociously at fifteen, from New Orleans to Southampton. Now she is "exiled" for her activity and is to go to Glacier National Park with her family. Basil wins an invitation to accompany her, only—turn again—to lose it by tooting his own horn insistently in her father's ear. Naturally, he is wild with grief. However, the last turn of all finds him reconciled to his fate and—read "because"—in renewed favor with Imogene Bissel, one of the hometown girls. The story is thus complicated by several reversals and has a certain interest because of them, but it lacks the ironic "bite" of "A Night at the Fair."

Basil is quite content to measure social success in terms of snobbery and material values similar to those governing life at St. Regis. However, the community is large enough to allow some apparent freedom despite parochial tenets. Hence the snobbery and materialism are neither questioned nor emphasized. And one is moved, as in "A Night at the Fair," by Fitzgerald's sensitive evocation of the quality of life in middle America. For example, Basil and Joe Gorman decide to walk around the block in their pyjamas:

> The sidewalk was warm to their bare feet. It was only midnight, but the square was deserted save for their whitish figures, inconspicuous against the starry darkness. They snorted with glee at their daring. Once a shadow, with loud human shoes, crossed the street far ahead, but the sound served only to increase their own unsubstantiality. Slipping quickly through the clearings made by gas lamps among the trees, they rounded the block, hurrying when they neared the Gorman house as though they had been really lost in a mid-summer night's dream.
>
> Up in Joe's room, they lay awake in the darkness.

And there is the delicious sureness of the dialogue. Trickling snatches of song, splashed with squirts of adolescent laughter:

> "No, look out. You'll break it. Bay-zil!"
> "Rip-lee!"
> "Sure I did!"
> Laughter
> "Going to the lake tomorrow?"
> "Going Friday."
> "Elwood's home."
> "Is Elwood Home?"
> "—you have broken my heart—"

"Look out now!"
"Look out!"

Basil and Minnie get into a motorboat and sit close together murmuring:

> "This fall—" "when you come to New Orleans
> —" "When I go to Yale year after next—" "When
> I come North to School—" "When I get back
> from Glacier Park—" "Kiss me once more." . . .
> "you're terrible. Do you know you're terrible: . . .
> You're absolutely terrible—"

Preoccupied all his life with the question of the relationship between money and the realization of a dream, Fitzgerald had been constantly aware, at the Newman School, of being "one of the poorest boys at a rich boys' school." "Forging Ahead" places that concern upon Basil in the financially uncertain summer before his anticipated departure for Yale, the emotional equivalent of Fitzgerald's Princeton.

> Yale was the far-away East, that he had loved with
> a vast nostalgia since he had first read books about
> great cities. Beyond the dreary railroad stations of
> Chicago and the night fires of Pittsburgh, back in
> the old states, something went on that made his
> heart beat fast with excitement. He was attuned
> to the fast, breathless bustle of New York, to the
> metropolitan days and nights that were tense as
> singing wires. Nothing needed to be imagined
> there, for it was all the very stuff of romance—life
> was as vivid and satisfactory as in books and
> dreams.
> But first, as a sort of gateway to that deeper,
> richer life, there was Yale.

Yale is important to Basil, as Princeton was to Fitzgerald—and in the same way. So when his mother loses her money—significantly enough, Basil is fatherless—Basil attempts to secure the dream by dream techniques: he reads Horatio Alger—*Bound to Rise*—and makes plans—dream plans—to work his way through Yale. Ultimately, he falls into the hands of Ben Reilly, wholesale drug baron, and his unscrupulous wife and daughter, killers of the dream, who manipulate Basil's private life, coercing him into service as a regular escort for unpopular Rhoda Reilly as a condition of employment. Obviously, Basil has made a mistake. What he should have done was to follow the advice of his practical neighbor Eddie Parmelee, who is going to State U. with Mr. Utsonomia, the grotesquely opportunistic Japanese whose vision of the deeper, richer life is a travesty of Basil's dream.

Eddie counsels Basil:

> "Here's what you ought to do," he said: "You borrow two thousand dollars from your mother and buy twenty shares in Ware Plow and Tractor. Then go to a bank and borrow two thousand more with those shares. Then you sit back for a year, and after that you won't have to think about earning your way through Yale."

That is the voice of the future. It is the voice of the finance capitalist who will come to dominate American business, speculating in paper without regard for anything but monetary gain. But it effectively eliminates Yale "as a sort of gateway" to a future shaped, in part, by Basil's own development, not simply accepted as the inevitable result of the way things are. And Basil cannot heed the advice. Nor does he need to. For his mother makes a $400,000 coup in a land deal, thereby preserving the dream. And that is, in a sense, "Forging Ahead."

"Basil and Cleopatra" gives us Basil at Yale, fulfilling Fitzgerald's unrequited hopes of becoming a football hero and reliving his bitter memories of misprised love. It is not one of the better stories, but it does have at least one marvelous line. When Minnie Bibble, the flirtatious Cleopatra, is begged for a kiss by Basil while she has another suitor on the hook, her response is: "I've stopped kissing people, Basil. Really, I'm too old; I'll be seventeen next May."

Basil is seventeen, too, in this story, an age when, as Fitzgerald says elsewhere, "one is a sort of counterfeit young man." And he is a counterfeit, staring up with "the practised eye of the commander" at windswept stars—"symbols of ambition, struggle and glory." Alas.

In "The Captured Shadow" he is a fifteen-year-old fledgling playwright, like Fitzgerald when his play of the same name was staged in St. Paul by Miss Elizabeth Magoffin's Elizabethan Dramatic Club. One of the notebooks that Fitzgerald kept contains the following observation:

> Fifteen is of all ages the most difficult to locate—to put one's fingers on and say, "That's the way I was." . . . all one can know is that somewhere between thirteen, boyhood's majority, and seventeen, when one is a sort of counterfeit young man, there is a time when youth fluctuates hourly between one world and another—pushed ceaselessly forward into unprecedented experiences and vainly trying to struggle back to the days when nothing had to be paid for. . . .

The story captures the fluctuations of adolescence. At one moment Basil is a boy with a sweet tooth and a penchant for self-dramatization; in the next, he is a burgeoning artist with some sense of responsibility and dramatic propriety.

The amateur theatrical is brought off splendidly, down to Miss Halliburton—Miss Magoffin's counterpart—"a pleasant person who combined the occupations of French teacher and bridge teacher, unofficial chaperon and children's friend, Basil felt that her superintendence would give the project an unprofessional ring." Best of all is the conclusion, where Basil confronts real value—for the play has been a success, an actual if minor accomplishment—and finds the absolute price that has to be paid for everything:

> . . . but it was already behind him. Even as the crowd melted away and the last few people spoke to him and went out, he felt a great vacancy come into his heart. It was over, it was done and gone— all that work, and interest and absorption. It was a hollowness like fear.

Priggishness triumphs in "A Woman With a Past," one of the Josephine stories, when Dudley Knowleton, who "has enough to do at New Haven serving on the committees and the team," returns to his piano-legged Adele, putting Josephine in her place—the arms of the first available Princeton man. That she has learned to distinguish between available and responsible men is supposed to be a mark of her maturation, but surely it is no more than an indication of a certain degree of shrewdness. Since Dudley is such a stick, perhaps even the shrewdness is open to question.

But a shrewdness or a worldly wiseness that enables her to see through pretentiousness and hypocrisy, to have her own headstrong way and to get back at women jealous, or men insufficiently appreciative, of her more or less open sensuousness is certainly one of the qualities that Fitzgerald saw in his first love, Ginevra King, upon whom Josephine and a host of other "new women" in his fiction were modeled. It is this quality that enables Josephine to drop—in both the hunterly and the other sense—her man in "First Blood." And it is this quality that infuriates Josephine's sister, whose prospective husband is almost seduced at the church steps in "A Nice Quiet Place." It is a quality that has within its range sheer bitchiness at one pole and at the other that desire for scope, for living the untrammeled life of a free spirit, which transcends worldly wiseness and abandons shrewdness in pursuit of a romantic ideal. Frequently the romantic ideal is trumpery—a blue-eyed fake in a chamois vest and a Byronic pose like Ridgeway Saunders in "A Nice Quiet Place." Or he may be an opera cape and a pose, like Travis de Coppet in "First Blood." Or like Dud Knowleton, the last man tapped for Skull and Bones, a prestigious Yale undergraduate club. For Fitzgerald remained very young at heart, almost until his heart gave out. Had he not, he would have forgotten that he'd loved and lost the rich and beautiful "speed" Ginevra King. And he never did. So she lives "forever young and still to be enjoyed" in Josephine.

2

Princeton and *Paradise*

Fitzgerald was admitted to Princeton on his seventeenth birthday, September 24, 1913. Like many undergraduates, his selection of a college had been made for a variety of reasons, none of them particularly academic. Football and the glamour of a musical comedy produced annually by the Triangle Club, a socially prestigious undergraduate organization at Princeton, had figured largely in his choice. He had played football at the Newman School, because, as Basil tells Lewis Crum in "The Freshest Boy," football is a way to make yourself "a lot more popular at school." Lewis goes into a rage at the implication that he is something less than popular. But Fitzgerald, like Basil, knew almost to a percentage point what his own current popularity standing was at any given moment. Having begun the game of striving for social position early, driven by the combined insecurities of his Fitzgerald-McQuillan heritage, he played it desperately, knowing as he did, that "popularity" is always expressed by a comparative and that success in the game is the result of constant application.

In addition to the prestige it provided, football, as played at Princeton in the era of the Big Three—Harvard, Yale, and Princeton—appealed to the romantic imagination of young Fitzgerald. He once said, "I think what started my Princeton sympathy was that they always just lost the football championship. Yale always seemed to nose them out in the last quarter by superior 'stamina' as the newspapers called it . . . . I imagined the Princeton men as slender and keen and romantic, and the Yale men as brawny and brutal and powerful."

But weighing only 138 pounds, Fitzgerald, however keen, was neither to gain prestige nor satisfy his romantic imagination by playing football. On the day of his admission to Princeton he had telegraphed his mother, asking her to send his football equipment "immediately." Twenty-three years later, he was still lamenting "the shoulder pads worn for one day on the Princeton freshman football field."

The Triangle Club was another matter. Fitzgerald had been writing since his early schooldays. During the two summers preceding his admission to Princeton, he'd had two plays produced in St. Paul by the Elizabethan Dramatic Club. Both "The Captured Shadow," a well-written piece about a gentleman burglar, and "The Coward," a Civil War melodrama, had been great successes. At the end of his freshman year at Princeton, he returned to St. Paul, where he wrote, produced, directed, and acted in a farce called "Assorted Spirits." It, too, was a success, achieving a second production at the exclusive White Bear Lake Yacht Club and making over three hundred dollars for the charity for which it had been staged. In the meantime, as a freshman, Fitzgerald had assisted in preparation for the annual production of the Triangle Club, which went on an extensive tour during Christmas vacation. And he started work on the book and lyrics for *Fie! Fie! Fi-Fi!*, a musical melodrama about a manicurist, a prime minister, and a gangster, which would be selected as the Triangle's next show and would go on tour as far west as Chicago and St. Louis. The show toured without Fitzgerald, however, for by that time his academic standing was so low that he had been declared ineligible for official participation.

So Fitzgerald spent the Christmas vacation at home, awaiting the arrival of a wealthy, willful Chicago beauty named Ginevra King, who was expected on a visit to friends of his in St. Paul. When she finally did arrive, on January 4, shortly before his departure for college, he was smitten with her at once and courted her assiduously in what little time he had left. Actually "courting" is something of a misnomer. It was more a contest, with each trying to impress the other by displays—or assertions—of experience, sophistication, worldliness, and daring. It was all rather childish. And Fitzgerald lost badly, as he was bound to do. For he had neither the wealth that gave Ginevra her assurance nor the arrogance that made each whim a categorical imperative and seemed, in one so young and beautiful, the charming essence of bold, free individualism. So Fitzgerald lost the contest and went back to Princeton in love with Ginevra, a love that he nourished by letter—her responses alone run to 227 pages—and, on at least one occasion, in New York, when "for one night . . . she made luminous the Ritz Roof on a brief passage through."

Later, Fitzgerald was to write a story called "Winter Dreams" in which Ginevra appears as Judy Jones. She was to appear in many of his stories, for he never forgot her. But in this one her essence is given its fullest scope, revealing

both its charm and its cruelty, displaying both the enchant-
ing and the terrible extremes of irresponsible individualism.

American higher education, which had been, historically, mainly a training ground for the professions, became
increasingly in the early years of this century, with little
or no change in curriculum, a preparation for a career as a
business executive. The expression, "It's not what you know,
but who you know" became less the response of an occasional disappointed cynic than the idea of a university for
young men on the rise. Of course, a career in business was
not completely incompatible with a nodding acquaintance
with the life of the mind, and at Harvard, for example,
Babbitt's sons learned to nod. But at Princeton accomplishment more often meant wearing the right clothes,
knowing the right people, and being named to the right
clubs. So Fitzgerald buttoned down his Brooks Brothers
collars, imitated the big men on campus, and accepted a bid
to Cottage, one of the more exclusive eating clubs that at
Princeton took the place of the Greek letter fraternities in
determining the hierarchy of social acceptability. He was
also rewarded for his efforts at Triangle by being made secretary. And he was elected to the editorial board of *The
Tiger*, a Princeton undergraduate newspaper.

But his success was short-lived. Malaria—possibly, too,
the first undiagnosed bout of several that he had with T.B.
—and poor grades combined to cheat him of the mark he
had hoped to make as a big man at Princeton, and he was
forced to withdraw in November of his junior year and return to St. Paul. He was to describe the year that brought
the debacle later in his journal as "a year of terrible disappointments and the end of all college dreams." Certainly
he felt the disappointment keenly. Worse, it helped to fix

that sense of insecurity that was already considerably developed in him before he entered Princeton. But in some ways the experience was not such a terrible one. For one thing, Fitzgerald did return to do his junior year over, displaying thereby the kind of fortitude that would serve him well as a writer and as a man. For another, upon his return his collegiate career took a new turn. Embittered by what he considered the unfairness of the college in penalizing him for academic insufficiency while embodying as an institution those very social goals for which he had striven, he turned away from those goals.

Fitzgerald had known Edmund Wilson, the man who was to become one of America's outstanding literary critics and men of letters, when he was "Bunny" Wilson, "the shy little scholar of Holder Court" and co-worker with Fitzgerald on a Triangle musical. Now he visited Wilson in New York, where Wilson had moved upon graduation from Princeton, and he began to associate with Wilson's intellectual friends at Princeton—John Biggs, Jr., who was later to be a judge, and John Peale Bishop, the future poet and scholar. From the latter, especially, he began to learn something of the seriousness of literature as a discipline and as an art rather than as sheer entertainment. He also consorted with younger men like Henry Slater, who read Tolstoi and Whitman and undertook a partially successful attack on the snobbish undergraduate eating clubs. He read more and more widely. And his writing for the *Nassau Literary Magazine* took on a new seriousness. Later he was to say, "I got nothing out of my first two years [at Princeton] —in the last I got my passionate love for poetry and historical perspective and ideas in general (however superficially), that carried me full swing into my career."

The first arc of that swing was completed on March

26, 1920, when Fitzgerald was twenty-three, with the publication of *This Side of Paradise*. By that time he had left Princeton, where he had begun the first version of the novel. He had enlisted in the United States Army, where as "the world's worst second lieutenant," according to a comrade in arms, he trained at several bases in the Midwest and South for anticipated service overseas in World War I and rewrote the book, then named *The Romantic Egotist*, "on the consecutive weekends of three months"—actually, he took five months. And he had met and fallen in love with Zelda Sayre, a lively, beautiful, and extremely popular girl from Montgomery, Alabama. In 1920 he would marry Zelda and sweep her off to New York, where they were to live like the fairy-tale prince and princess of some absurd dream of the twenties, all aglitter with gold and glory for a year and a day or two. But first, he must secure the dream, for Zelda, like Fitzgerald himself, wanted not mere association with glittering things but the glittering things themselves. And after another revision, back in St. Paul, his manuscript had been accepted for publication by Charles Scribner's Sons, and the dream secured.

Actually the book itself has a dreamlike quality, which derives, in part, from its fragmented, episodic character, for it is as little structured as a spilled glass of champagne. Indeed, it is one of the most ill-written books of any that has ever achieved fame, from its spelling to its characterization, from its diction to its design, from its puerile intellectual posturing to its excruciating poetizing. Fitzgerald's friend Edmund Wilson described it well when, reviewing it in *The Bookman*, he said:

> [Amory Blaine] was . . . an uncertain quantity in a phantasmagoria of incident which had no dominating intention to endow it with unity and force

. . . . [*This Side of Paradise*] is very immaturely
imagined: it is always just verging on the ludicrous. And, finally, it is one of the most illiterate
books of any merit ever published . . . . It is not
only full of bogus ideas and faked literary refer-
ences but it is full of English words misused with
the most reckless abandon.

Wilson might have gone further—in fact, he did, in a
letter to Fitzgerald—for the book not only verges on the
ludicrous, it frequently topples over into it, as, for example,
when the devil appears, all unprepared for, in shoes "with
the little ends curling up," as a sample of the "unutterably
terrible."

This Side of Paradise is an adolescent book in the fullest sense of the word. It is about and by one. And it contains all of the awkwardness and confusion, the brashness
and uncertainty, the idealism and pretentiousness, the
energy and bad taste, of that particular period in a young
man's life. It is a bad book, but it rings true. Like an ill-
minted coin, it is unsatisfactory but not counterfeit.

The novel tells the story of Amory Blaine from earli-
est youth, as the spoiled darling of his affected, neurasthenic
mother, through school years at St. Regis and college at
Princeton, with a brief interlude as a training-camp soldier
at the end of World War I. It ends with the young man,
disappointed in a love affair with the beautiful Rosalind
Connage—which terminates unsatisfactorily—seeking direction and meaning for his life in the confusing postwar
world of the twenties.

Irreverent toward the attitudes and values of an earlier
day, which were centered in a work ethic and rigidly, if
somewhat hypocritically, moralistic, the book celebrates
the freedom of newly independent youth. At a time when

the generation gap was beginning to widen and more young people were going to college than ever before, Amory and his friends at Princeton, where most of the action of the novel takes place, are leisured young skeptics, more concerned with art, alcohol, and amour than with work and Holy Writ. The book was thus heady wine to the young and caught on like wildfire, quickly becoming a big seller.

And there are good things in it. Many of the college experiences have an authentic tone. There is, for example, the night at the end of their sophomore year when Amory and Tom D'Invilliers borrow bicycles and ride out into the dark countryside, past "the sleeping school of Lawrenceville," analyzing themselves and one another with romantic seriousness in hopeless clichés. How satisfying such intimate concern and such simplification is!

> "It's good, this ride, isn't it?" Tom said presently.
> "Yes; it's a good finish, it's knock-out; everything's good tonight. Oh, for a hot, languorous summer and Isabelle!"
> ". . . let's say some poetry."
> So Amory declaimed "The Ode to a Nightingale" to the bushes they passed.

And they ride back through the night to the tune of more self-analysis and hurry "to the refreshment of a shower that would have to serve in place of sleep," into the bright day of a gaudy class reunion with its alumni-crowded streets, bright costumes, banners, noise, and a scattering of gray-haired men, sitting talking quietly while the panorama sweeps by.

Or there is Amory and Tom's farewell to Princeton, as they roam the campus, pausing to watch "the moon rise, to make silver of the slate roof of Dodd and blue the rustling trees."

"The grass is full of ghosts tonight," says Amory. "The whole campus is alive with them."

> "The torches are out," whispered Tom. "Ah, Messalina, the long shadows are building minarets on the stadium—"
> For an instant the voices of freshman year surged around them and they looked at each other with faint tears in their eyes.
> "Damn!"
> "Damn!"

Corn. But pure corn.

More compelling, doubtless, is the automobile crash in which Dick Humbird, a Princeton classmate, is killed. Framed by an alumni reunion and a college dance, the episode is as unexpected as an accident, as vivid as a widening circle of blood in the street, lit by a roadside arc light. It is brief and immediate, beginning with the jolting stop of a second car, full of half-drunk revelers like the first. There is the wrecked car. Forms lying in the road. Recognition.

> . . . they turned the form over.
> "It's Dick—Dick Humbird!"
> "Oh, Christ!"
> "Feel his heart!"
> . . . .
> "He's . . . dead, all right."

Then doctors. A sheet to cover the body. Other injured boys. And the drive back to Princeton.

But for all its brevity, the episode is fully orchestrated and has resonance. There is a harpy in an old kimona to announce the terrible event. Injured Sloane, one of the party, reminds us of the regular course of life behind the accident with his delirious recollection of a chemistry lecture he must attend at 8:10. And a mangled cat from some alley of Amory's childhood connects the death with all others before Amory steps out of the house to which the body is carried into "the late night wind—a wind that stirred a broken fender on the mass of bent metal to a plaintive, tinny sound," a tinny sound that echoes the cracked hollowness of the old crone's voice that announced the event.

In quite a different mode, but also effective, is an excursion to Asbury Park. Beginning with Alec Connage's waking of Amory—"Wake up, Original Sin, and scrape yourself together. Be in front of Renwick's in half an hour. Somebody's got a car."—it runs the gamut of undergraduate high jinks with infectious enthusiasm, mixing poetry and buffoonery in a raffish cavalcade over boardwalk and beaches, through restaurants, theaters, and shops, in a modern-day spring pilgrimage not unlike Chaucer's, until "Sunday broke stolid and respectable, and . . . they returned to Princeton via the Fords of transient farmers, and broke up with colds in their heads, but otherwise none the worse for wandering."

An epic jaunt, the episode anticipates Amory's epic binge later in the book, which begins in the Knickerbocker Bar in New York City, under the beaming eye of Maxfield Parrish's mural "Old King Cole." Amory is trying to forget his rejection by Rosalind, the sister of a college friend, with whom he is in love. As he puts it drunkenly, "Cel'brating blowmylife. Great moment blow my life. Can't tell you 'bout it—" The effort is made with the aid of alcohol, of course, and Fitzgerald touches all the steps of a drunk's progress.

There is anger, as a companion, trying to restrain him, mutters, "You've had plenty, old boy."

> Amory eyed him dumbly until Wilson grew embarrassed under the scrutiny.
> "Plenty hell!" said Amory finally. "I haven't had a drink today."

Tipsy philosophy:

> "S a mental was'e," he insisted with owl-like wisdom. "Two years my life spent inalleshual vacuity. Los' idealism, got be physcal anmal," he shook his fist expressively at Old King Cole, "got be Prussian 'bout ev'thing, women 'specially, Use' be straight 'bout women college. Now don' givadam." He expressed his lack of principle by sweeping a seltzer bottle with a broad gesture to noisy extinction on the floor, but this did not interrupt his speech. "Seek pleasure where find it for tomorrow die! 'At's philosophy for me now on."

Dipsomaniacal gallantry:

> Someone mentioned that a famous cabaret star was at the next table, so Amory rose and, approaching gallantly, introduced himself . . . this involved him in an argument, first with her escort and then with the headwaiter—Amory's attitude being a lofty and exaggerated courtesy. . . .

Maudlin sentiment:

> "We were so happy," he intoned dramatically, "so very happy." Then he gave way again and knelt beside the bed, his head half-buried in the pillow.
> "My own girl-my own— Oh—"

Drunken reasonableness:

> "But listen, Amory, you're making yourself sick.
> You're white as a ghost."
> Amory considered the question. He tried to look
> at himself in the mirror but even by squinting up
> one eye could only see as far as the row of bottles
> behind the bar.
> "Like som'n solid. We go get some—some
> salad."

There is a fight, a near riot, several drunken flirta-
tions, intermittent sleep in improbable places, a suicide
attempt (or the announcement of a projected one), endless
arguments; Amory gets lost, beaten, ejected from a bar, and
fired from his job. Three weeks and countless quarts later,
with a black eye and a swollen jaw, he finds himself "over
the first flush of pain" and sobering up, on the first day of
Prohibition.

Moreover, the snippets that I have culled for illustration are not isolated fragments, deliberately selected for
purposes of "balance." There is, as I've suggested, something authentic about the book as a whole. The nostalgic
presentation of a sentimentally conceived, song-filled campus appropriately reflects bourgeois experience early in the
century. The superficial traffic in half-baked "ideas" is representative of undergraduate intellectual life then, now, and
probably always. The gauche efforts at social adjustment,
the snobbery, the experiments in sexuality, the clannish-
ness, and the sense of adolescent camaraderie are poignant
reminders of significant aspects of youth. And the tone of
boyish bravado is a universal expression of the continuing
war between the generations. Beyond all that, there is a
feeling in the book for the sense of ferment in a time when
widely accepted values were rapidly changing on a wide

scale after a long period of stability. There is a hectic flush to the life, a sense of dislocation in the characters, a frenzied activity, a wildness in the gaiety. And beneath it all, like a perpetual sob in the throat, a pervasive sadness indicative of widespread displacement, uncertainty, alienation.

How then is it a bad book? It is bad principally in its inability to hold its various richnesses together. It lacks a sense of direction and order, or shape. This is felt mainly in the characters, whom Fitzgerald had not completely conceived. Early in the book, for example, Amory has a conversation with Monsignor D'Arcy. The Monsignor, patterned on Fitzgerald's friend and counselor, Father Fay, is a theatrical character combining elements that might be thought to appeal to the adolescent: mild paradox, a touch of decadent aestheticism, arrogance, whimsy, a show of profundity, sensitivity. But none of these qualities register as inherent in the character. They appear as applied colors, unskillfully laid on by an immature boy. As a result, Monsignor D'Arcy is grotesque, unbelievable, a travesty of the man he is supposed to be. Thus when he refers to the "divine irony of the 'Agamemnon,' " one can't believe that he ever read Aeschylus. When he converses with the worldly Thornton Hancock by way of educating Amory, no real conversation takes place. What we have instead is a boy's silly impression of a dialogue deeply, deeply deep. And since the boy himself is involved in the conversation, such as it is, and weighed by the speakers in terms of his putative contribution, the result is farcical. Thinking of Amory at the conclusion of the section of the book called "Code of the Young Egotist," Thornton Hancock says, "He's a radiant boy!" One's response is "My God, how could he know?"

Reflecting on the female characters in the book, one is

reminded of Ezra Pound's image of Maent, in "Near Perigord": "a broken bundle of mirrors." However, in Pound's relatively short poem the complexity of the woman is condensed in the image. In *This Side of Paradise* Myra and Isabelle, Clara, and Rosalind, and Eleanor are scattered fragments of what was perhaps felt by the author as facets of a single image, but they are incompletely conceived. And one can't be sure of what the total image was supposed to be. One can resort to psychoanalysis and suggest reasons for the fragmented female. But there is not enough in the book to hold the parts together as a whole or to allow them to walk in the road of the novel on their own, as Flaubert tells us good mirrors should.

These female characters are, of course, presented with varying degrees of success. Myra, briefly sketched, is Amory's first schoolboy encounter with the opposite sex. Petulant and ungrammatical, she is seen from a mildly satirical point of view:

> "You're such a funny boy," puzzled Myra.
>
> "How d'y' mean?" Amory gave immediate attention, on his own ground at last.
>
> "Oh—always talking about crazy things. Why don't you come ski-ing with Marylyn and I tomorrow?"
>
> "I don't like girls in the daytime," he said shortly, and then, thinking this a bit abrupt, he added: "But I like you." He cleared his throat. "I like you first and second and third."
>
> Myra's eyes became dreamy. What a story this would make to tell Marylyn! Here on the couch with this *wonderful*-looking boy—the little fire— the sense that they were alone in the great building.

Myra capitulated, the atmosphere was too appropriate.

"I like you the first twenty-five," she confessed, her voice trembling, "and Froggy Parker twenty-sixth."

On the whole, she is a convincing if somewhat coyly conceived junior version of the pampered and self-indulgent upper-middle-class woman seeking thrills surreptitiously and retreating behind a screen of convention or authority when danger threatens. What is curious is Amory's sudden change of attitude toward her. For after kissing her, he is inexplicably filled with loathing, which seems excessive, and passionately rejects her perfectly normal and predictable advances. (Later in the book a chorus girl named Axia is similarly to trigger Amory's inconsistent priggishness when a proffered glass of brandy calls up the devil in a thoroughly unconvincing way.)

With Isabelle the coyly satirical element disappears. Patterned directly on Ginevra King, Isabelle is the collegiate version of the new woman, passionately pursuing pleasure and capable of saying "Damn!" when thwarted. To be sure, the passion is rather tame, its manifestation being purely osculatory. But the intention here is to celebrate the hard-boiled virgin, though the nominative aspect of the phenomenon is rather more evident than the adjectival.

Clara, based on Fitzgerald's widowed young cousin Cecilia, might be described as a soft-boiled virgin. Capable of smoking and of discussing sex, she is a safe nod in the direction of the emancipated woman, insulated for Fitzgerald by kinship and for Amory by her "precious babies," an asserted but unbelievable aspect of her sentimentalized domesticity.

Rosalind is, doubtless, the most fully presented woman in *This Side of Paradise*. A sister of Amory's Princeton classmate Alec Connage, she is both a great beauty and a free spirit. Rich, willful, witty—after a fashion—and enormously popular, she reigns imperiously, discarding admirers with indifference, manipulating her stuffy proper parents, who want to marry her off to the highest bidder, and falling in love with Amory. To be sure, her actual relationship with Amory is rather tiresome, consisting as it does of a repeated exchange of strained aphorisms demonstrating how "advanced" each of the participants is. But it is meant to be true love, and no doubt reflects the strained intensity of Fitzgerald's engagement to Zelda. Indeed, the episode is centered in Fitzgerald's profoundest fear at the time he was rewriting *This Side of Paradise*: that Zelda would reject him because he hadn't enough money to support the kind of glamorous life she aspired to. Turning Amory away finally, Rosalind says:

> . . . I like sunshine and pretty things and cheerful-
> ness—and I dread responsibility. I don't want to
> think about pots and kitchens and brooms. I want
> to worry whether my legs will get slick and brown
> when I swim in the summer.

The attitude is, of course, a childish one. But it is not inconsistent with the character of either Amory or Rosalind, nor is it inconsistent with their prototypes, Scott Fitzgerald and Zelda Sayre. To be sure, Fitzgerald's "spoiled priest" trait, the trait that resulted in an occasional unmotivated priggishness in an otherwise worldly, liberated Amory, enables him to see the bitch goddess lurking in the irresponsible hedonist. One sentence in Rosalind's tear-stained, hysterical farewell to Amory reveals her as actually battening on his suffering. Saying good-bye to her suffering, broken-hearted lover, she cautions: "Don't ever forget me, Amory—"

However, Rosalind is based on Zelda, whom he was only much later to understand he loved "not wisely but too well." So in the novel the bitch goddess is Eleanor, another character. And even in her the quality is only intermittently apparent, evil leering out quite unconvincingly from the green eyes of a sophomoric sprite whom Amory ludicrously equates with the Dark Lady of Shakespeare's *Sonnets,* and Fitzgerald melodramatically equips with a mad mother and an equestrian impulse toward suicide. For the most part, Eleanor is stagey romanticism and bad poetry. From the haystack in the thunderstorm to the short walk back from the cold hillside, with Amory's love waning slowly—but not too slowly—with the waning moon, the episode involving her is preposterously unconvincing. "La Belle Dame sans Merci" is hidden somewhere in the women of *This Side of Paradise,* but she is too much overlaid with sentiment and phony trappings, too ill-conceived to be felt as a significant force in the book. She will reappear, however, in later works more convincingly portrayed.

As to the theme of *This Side of Paradise,* that seems to me to be equally unclear. The first part, taking its title from Fitzgerald's first draft of the novel, is called "The Romantic Egotist"; the second is called "The Education of a Personage." The concept of a personage is based on Monsignor D'Arcy's rather cloudy attempt to distinguish between a personality and a personage in a long talk he has with Amory early in the book. Presumably the novel is concerned with the growth of a romantic egotist, the mere personality, into a true personage. But the distinction between them lacks clarity of definition. There is little in Monsignor D'Arcy's illustrations of the latter to distinguish it from the former. The novel ends with Amory's declaration, "I know myself . . . but that is all." Of course, if Socrates can be believed, that is considerable. But if that is the smug implication of the conclusion, it is thoroughly misleading. For Amory is so fragmented a character, so incompletely comprehended by his author, so much a creature of contradictory impulse and incantatory rhetoric as to have no knowable self. "Grown up to find all Gods dead, all wars fought, all faiths in man shaken . . . ," he still finds it in himself somehow to "accept what was acceptable, roam, grow, rebel, sleep deep through many nights. . . ." "Safe now, free from all hysteria" and sorry for the "muddled, unchastened world" which still feeds "romantically on mistakes and half-forgotten dreams," he is "not sorry for himself." Yet he broods over "unrealized dreams," and crying out, "Oh, Rosalind! Rosalind! . . . ," he asserts, "It's all a poor substitute at best." ("It" is for Amory the whole complex of dreams and accomplishments, the world he might inherit, but is content to lose for love.) He will, nevertheless, use himself to the utmost in the service of something. And as he goes forth into the new day of a rhetorical climax, stretching "his arms toward the crystalline, radiant sky," he forgets that he was destined a dozen or so lines earlier "to go out into that dirty gray turmoil" that was the reflex of another mood.

Mingling schoolboy socialism and speciously aristocratic contempt for the masses, aestheticism and devotion to a journalistic conception of hard reality, trumpery intellectual gamesmanship and the attitude of a man about town, youthful idealism and childish cynicism, worldliness and naiveté, all interlarded with a thick impasto of sentimentality and varnished with a heavy coating of poetizing, Amory Blaine's portrait is, to say the least, unclear. And the book, for all its insights, for all its patches of brilliance and authenticity of tone, remains unclear, too.

"Well," says Fitzgerald's epigraph from Rupert Brooke, "this side of Paradise! . . . There's little comfort in the wise." Are we to take the expression as a lament for our lost state or a celebration of innocent ignorance? Presumably the latter, for Fitzgerald has a second epigraph, from Oscar Wilde, to reinforce the first: "Experience is the name so many people give to their mistakes." But what then of the progress of the superficial personality toward the state where he becomes a personage? And what of the self-knowledge that Amory proclaims himself the master of as the book ends? Are we to chalk up both to experience or to write off both as mistakes? Since neither progress nor self-knowledge has been demonstrated, I think we must conclude that Fitzgerald was uncertain himself and await the surer development in the later books of the moralist Fitzgerald knew himself to be.

3

Death of Fear

In a letter to his daughter Scottie, written in 1938, Fitz-gerald says:

> When I was your age, I lived with a great dream. The dream grew and I learned how to speak of it and to make people listen. Then the dream divided one day when I decided to marry your mother after all, even though I knew she was spoiled and meant no good to me. I was sorry immediately I had married her, but being patient in those days, made the best of it and got to love her in another way. You came along and for a long time we had quite a lot of happiness out of our lives. But I was a man divided—she wanted me to work too much for *her* and not enough for my dream.

The letter is a shockingly bitter one, in which he rails at Scottie because of some trouble she got into at her school. And it was, of course, written just two years before Fitzgerald's death, when he was sick and working hard to rebuild a reputation as a writer that had by then vanished almost completely. The early days of his marriage were eighteen years in the past, and his memory of them was, doubtless, colored by the calamitous events of the intervening years. But the letter points to a division that was real and that unquestionably affected him, even before he permitted himself to recognize it consciously. For he was "spoiled" himself, as the moralist in him, the "spoiled priest," was to recognize. And he encouraged and responded to self-indulgent excess in Zelda even as he reveled in it himself, lamenting the while at the toll it exacted of him as a writer, and, increasingly, attributing that toll to Zelda's demands.

But the demands were not Zelda's alone. Partly they were the product of Fitzgerald's desire "to enjoy, to be prodigal and open-hearted . . . to miss nothing." Now to miss nothing in the twenties in America required a considerable capacity for crude experience. As Fitzgerald said in "Early Success": "America was going on the greatest, gaudiest spree in history. . . . The whole golden boom was in the air—its splendid generosities, its outrageous corruptions and the tortuous death struggle of the old America in prohibition." Moreover, Fitzgerald had written *This Side of Paradise*, a book that was widely celebrated as a manifestation of the splendid generosity of youth involved in a struggle with the deadening restrictions and hypocrisy of older America. And he and Zelda were taken as exemplars of a new spirit—unconstrainedly devoted to the deliberate and energetic pursuit of pleasure, to "having fun" in a demonstratively adolescent fashion. So they lived at the Commodore Hotel in New York in a haze of alcohol and a perpetual round of parties, broken by sensational escapades—riding down Fifth Avenue on the top of taxicabs, swimming in the Plaza fountain, fighting with waiters, and dancing atop people's tables in restaurants.

But riding on top of taxicabs costs more than riding in them, as Zelda observed. And then there were the parties and the clothes and the alcohol. So Fitzgerald soon ran out of money. He recalls the shock of that discovery in an essay he wrote for *The Saturday Evening Post*, "How to Live on $36,000 a Year":

> . . . after we had been married for three months I found one day to my horror that I didn't have a dollar in the world, and the weekly hotel bill for two hundred dollars would be due next day. I remember the mixed feelings with which I issued from the bank on hearing the news.
>
> "What's the matter?" demanded my wife anxiously, as I joined her on the sidewalk. "You look depressed."
>
> "I'm not depressed," I answered cheerfully; "I'm just surprised. We haven't got any money."
>
> "Haven't got any money," she repeated calmly, and we began to walk up the Avenue in a sort of trance. "Well, let's go to the movies," she suggested jovially.
>
> It all seemed so tranquil that I was not a bit cast down. The cashier had not even scowled at me. I had walked in and said to him, " How much money have I got?" And he looked in a big book and answered, "None."
>
> That was all. There were no harsh words, no blows. And I knew that there was nothing to worry about. I was now a successful author, and when successful authors ran out of money all they had to do was sign cheques. I wasn't poor—they

couldn't fool me. . . . why, it was impossible that
I should be poor! I was living at the best hotel in
New York!

Finding themselves broke, the Fitzgeralds bought an
expensive car and drove to Connecticut, looking for a house
in which they could cut expenses and settle down, and
where Fitzgerald could get some writing done. They found a
house—in Westport—and miraculously Fitzgerald did get
some writing done. *The Beautiful and Damned*, published
in 1922, was largely written there. But they were unable
either to cut expenses or to settle down. In fact, their week-
end parties often stretched right through the week. And
when they weren't giving parties, they were going to them,
in New York, returning in the wee hours of the morning to
sleep off the effects of their revels on the Westport lawn,
where their Japanese butler would find them in the
morning.

Of course, the butler and the booze had to be paid for.
As did all the appurtenances of "the greatest, gaudiest spree
in history," including the trip to Europe which they decided to take when Fitzgerald completed *The Beautiful and
Damned* in the spring of 1921. That trip was a part of the
spree. And it was a dismal failure. France was "a bore and a
disappointment"; Italy, no better. And after ten days in
London, where they had planned to stay for some time,
they decided to cut short their trip and return home,
despite Edmund Wilson's urgent plea from Paris that they
cancel their passage and "come to Paris for the summer."

What else could Europe have been but a "bore and a
disappointment" to two adolescents on a spree, bent on
"having fun" in the most demonstrative and self-advertising
way? Even their meetings with respected literary figures
were marred by egocentric demonstrations. Anatole France,

whom they tried to track down like tourists hunting celebrities, managed to evade them. But John Galsworthy, whom they did meet, they embarrassed with fulsome praise. And James Joyce, in whose presence Fitzgerald attempted to jump out of a window to show his regard for the great writer, thought that "that young man must be mad." Charles Kingsley, Scribner's British representative, they simply used, borrowing money from him on short notice to buy tickets home. "What an overestimated place Europe is!" Fitzgerald concluded. And when Zelda later summarized the early days of her marriage, through the time of their return from Europe, in a fictionalized account in *Save Me the Waltz*, she characterized it thus:

> Lustily splashing their dreams in the dark pool of gratification, their fifty thousand dollars bought a cardboard baby-nurse for Bonnie, a second-hand Marmon, a Picasso etching, a white satin dress . . . a yellow chiffon dress . . . a dress as green as fresh wet paint, two white knickerbocker suits exactly alike, a broker's suit . . . and two first class tickets for Europe.

Bonnie is the fictional name for their daughter Scottie, who was born, following their return from Europe, in October. The Picasso etching is perhaps a nod in the direction of culture. And Zelda has left out the alcohol. Aside from that the list is an accurate, if ungrammatical, index of the Fitzgeralds' showy "gratification," a getting and spending relieved by two white gestures of defiance—women didn't wear pants suits then—and a bright green image fresh as paint.

To be sure, the bright image was Fitzgerald's *raison d'être*. And the gestures of defiance its necessary accompaniment. But the rest of the baggage, including the booze and the butler, came high. And, increasingly, it was bought at the expense of the image. For Fitzgerald soon learned that the popular magazines would buy cheap and shoddy stories, work that he was ashamed of, for a higher price than he could get for serious work. And, ashamed though he was, he ground them out and sold them. Later he would see such actions as betrayals of his artistic integrity, a selling out of his dream, occasioned by Zelda's extravagance and productive of an artistically disabling division within himself. But his attempt to account for this division is an oversimplification. For Zelda's extravagance and intemperance were but echoes of his own. Moreover, while these qualities were, in a sense, destructive of the artist's dream, they were also essential elements in it. For the artist was prodigal and openhearted, wanting to miss no part of the greatest, gaudiest spree in history. He was also an old-fashioned moralist. Advising his daughter about her own career, in a letter written in 1939, he says:

> . . . if you start any kind of a career following the footsteps of Cole Porter and Rogers and Hart, it might be an excellent try. Sometimes I wish I had gone along with that gang, but I guess I am too much a moralist at heart, and really want to preach at people in some acceptable form, rather than to entertain them.

He was right about the division of his dream, but wrong in attributing that division to Zelda. The division was in himself. It was a part of the dream.

Reflecting the split between sensualist and puritan, prodigal and moralist, entertainer and preacher, idealist and cynic, *The Beautiful and Damned* is about that self-division, an immobilizing self-division that has something of the frozen horror of a nightmare. However, unlike *This*

Side of Paradise, which is dreamlike in its fragmentary directionlessness, *The Beautiful and Damned* has an ostensible direction. It traces the degeneration of Anthony Patch from bright and witty man-about-town to drunken stumblebum, with an ironic semireversal at the end that leaves him a wealthy catatonic.

Handsome, sensitive, expensively educated, interested in the arts, capable of enjoying life, a man of sufficient presence to be attractive to the beautiful Gloria Gilbert, Anthony Patch is at the beginning of the book, like Fitzgerald himself, a rather prepossessing representative of his class. In fact, the very antithesis of the narrow-minded, moralistic Neanderthal of a grandfather, whose life has consisted in moneygrubbing, Anthony seems to provide fresh hope for a new way of life. Like Fitzgerald, too, Anthony wins the beautiful girl and sets out to enjoy life to the full. But Anthony fails, as Fitzgerald feared he might himself. Fitzgerald feared that he might not be able to provide for Zelda the kind of glamorous life that she—and he—desperately wanted. He feared that his talent might be dissipated; his work come to nothing; the glamorous alternative to the life of a moneygrubber fade like a bright-colored dream. In Anthony Patch he projects those fears, as they are realized, ironically, against a society in flux, while Anthony himself stands still or, in fact, regresses to the point where he resembles the grandfather whom he despised.

Fitzgerald dedicated *The Beautiful and Damned* to Shane Leslie, George Jean Nathan, and Maxwell Perkins—two writer friends and his editor at Scribner's—with appreciation for "much literary help and encouragement." And it is evident that he has learned something about plot, about how a novel should progress from beginning to end, from his literary helpers. He is still overly addicted to headlines, compartmentalizing observations in the manner of an undergraduate essayist under such rubrics as "The Reproachless Apartment," "Three Men," "A Lady's Legs," "The Diary," "Two Young Women," and "Signlight and Moonlight." And his fondness for drawing-room comedy dialogue compels him to indulge periodically in artificially set-off dramatic conversations. When these conversations are good, they're not so very good. And when they're bad, they're howlers. This is particularly true when the dialogue personifies abstractions, as it does, for example, in "A Flash-Back in Paradise," where "Beauty" and "The Voice" exchange bromides to no particular purpose. However, despite these unfortunate intrusions, the characters are more fully blocked in than they are in *This Side of Paradise*. They are better developed and more solid, and one has a sense of their unfolding—growing or coming apart. To some degree this sense of development is the result of Fitzgerald's concern with the passing of time, the loss of youth. Thus the flawless Gloria, Anthony's beautiful siren and later his wife, develops wrinkles. The effects of alcohol on Anthony reduce a lithe young man to flabby middle age before his time, with a paunch, red-veined eyes, and the shakes. As for Anthony's friends, the writer Dick Caramel's lumpy face fills out while his shelves fill up with trashier and trashier products of his ever active pen. And Maury Noble, the intellectual, falls from his perch of philosophical indifference into the slough of snobbishness.

But there is more to the book than a simple tracing of the inevitable process of aging. As a matter of fact, Joseph Bloeckman, who first appears as a stereotyped Jewish movie magnate on the rise, vying with Anthony for Gloria Gilbert's attention, develops dignity and stature as the novel unfolds. Or rather, one should say that Anthony becomes aware of Bloeckman's inherent dignity as his own Patchy dignity falls from him. For Bloeckman, when he is first introduced, is described by Fitzgerald as "a dignified man and a proud one." But he had begun his career as a peanut vendor with a traveling circus, had been a sideshow ballyhoo man and, later, the proprietor of a second-class vaudeville house. His wealth is the consequence of "nagging financial ambitions." And, of course, he is Jewish. So Anthony sees him as an underdone man, "boiled-looking." He has "a little too evident assurance" for Anthony, who feels himself to the manner born because his money is a generation old. And Bloeckman makes mistakes. He praises Anthony's grandfather as "a fine example of an American" while Anthony deplores old "Cross Patch's" unsophisticated moralizing. He talks about college hockey victories when nobody a year or two out of an Ivy League college heeds any college athletic event but two or three big football games. So he's treated with "faint and ironic chill." And since there is no hint of understanding in Bloeckman's manner, Anthony is permitted superiorly to wonder whether or not he "received the intended impression."

About halfway through the book, however, when Anthony, now married to Gloria, meets Bloeckman by chance, he seems to have grown tremendously in dignity. "The boiled look was gone," Anthony observes, "he seemed 'done' at last." Of course, part of this change is merely one of appearance. But, naturally, Anthony would notice that. He notices also that Bloeckman is no longer overdressed, that his ties are "right," that he has abandoned his rings and does without the "raw glow of a manicure." But he also notices, and it is a sign of the disintegration of his own personality, that "this dignity appeared also in his personality." Bloeckman has acquired reticence, aloofness, weight instead of bulk, and Anthony "no longer felt a correct superiority in his presence."

Later still, Bloeckman reappears after a year's absence, and we are told, "The process of general refinement was still in progress—always he dressed a little better, his intonation was mellower, and in his manner there was perceptibly more assurance that the fine things of the world were his by a natural and inalienable right."

Of course, one of the fine things of the world, at least in appearance, is Gloria. And Bloeckman does not have her. But Gloria and Anthony have been wildly extravagant. Anthony's grandfather has not conveniently died, as they hoped he would, leaving them his tremendous fortune. Their marriage has had some shocks, and they have both come to see through the glossy veneer of each other's personalities to the plain wood beneath. When Bloeckman offers Gloria the possibility of a glamorous movie career, she is tempted to accept. Anthony refuses, however, to permit her to do so, and she reluctantly declines the offer. Significantly "neither of them ever mentioned the probability that Bloeckman was by no means disinterested, but they knew that it lay back of Anthony's objection."

The key word in the sentence quoted above is "probability." For neither of them really knows what Bloeckman's motives are, yet both of them suspect, their suspicion being an index of their own increasing pettiness. As it transpires, when the once haughty Gloria, humbled by financial insecurity and marital frustrations, later goes secretly to

Bloeckman, seeking a screen test, she is neither seduced by Bloeckman, nor gets the coveted job. She has begun to show signs of age; she is offered a character part instead.

Finally even Anthony becomes indifferent to her. The ultimate sign of his degeneration is his request that Gloria go to Bloeckman for money to satisfy his craving for alcohol. She refuses to do so, and in one of the most terrible scenes in the book, Anthony traces Bloeckman to a nightclub, where the now coolly self-assured Jew, completely assimilated into the society from which Anthony has fallen, in recognition of which he has changed his name from Bloeckman to Black, confronts the broken scion of Wasp authority. Anthony accuses Bloeckman of having kept his wife out of the movies, and when Bloeckman upbraids him for his drunken insolence, he calls him a "Goddam Jew." Bloeckman knocks him off his feet with a blow in the mouth, and then has him thrown out of the club as a blackmailing bum.

Bloeckman's role in the novel is, therefore, a complex one. His growth as a character is actually a revelation of inherent worth as seen, progressively more fully, through the eyes of his declining rival for a prize that alters as he approaches it, even as he alters in approaching it. Thus the society, which he changes his name to become a fixture in, is anti-Semitic in tone. But while Gloria calls him "Blockhead," she no longer adorns the society that he flourishes in under the name of Black. And when Anthony calls him a "Goddam Jew," that is both a sign of Anthony's ultimate decline and a signal for Bloeckman to assert his new-won authority.

The evolution of Bloeckman's authority is, in an important sense, an index of the sweeping social change the novel documents. Fitzgerald points to these changes early in the novel. Commenting on the inauguration of a new social season, when debutantes come out, at the beginning of Chapter Two, Fitzgerald reflects a city in flux:

> Three dozen virtuous females of the first layer [he notes] were proclaiming their fitness . . . to bear children unto three dozen millionaires. Five dozen virtuous females of the second layer were proclaiming not only this fitness, but in addition a tremendous undaunted ambition toward the first three dozen young men, who were of course invited to each of the ninety-six parties—as were the young lady's group of family friends, acquaintances, college boys, and eager young outsiders. To continue, there was a third layer from the skirts of the city . . . and doubtless contiguous layers down to the city's shoes: Jewesses were coming out into a society of Jewish men and women, from Riverside to the Bronx, and looking forward to a rising young broker or jeweller and a kosher wedding; Irish girls were casting their eyes, with a license at last to do so, upon a society of young Tammany politicians, pious undertakers, and grown-up choir-boys.

Even poor girls wrapping soap in the factories dream of a coveted male who will free them from their drudgery, providing them with the "spectacular excitement" of social mobility.

"The City was coming out!" Fitzgerald concludes. His comprehensive little catalogue of the ways in which it was doing so is edged by the snobbery of Anthony Patch, whose point of view it is close to. But there is excitement, too, in this recognition of a vast coming out, this view of a city and a society in flux. And even Anthony participates in this movement, despite his snobbery. For his own life is, in part, a celebration of the pursuit of youthful pleasure and a rejection of the moral order of old Adam Patch, an old Adam whose morality is the hidebound and hypocritical life- and joy-extinguishing morality of Anthony Comstock, the mono-maniacal reformer who "levelled . . . body-blows at liquor, literature, vice, art, patent medicines, and Sunday theatres," indifferently. In fact, one of the principal ironies of the novel accrues from the circumstance that Anthony's pursuit of pleasure is ultimately as life-denying as old Adam's principles, and at the end of the book he finally inherits, through a kind of poetic justice, the millions left by his fabulously wealthy grandfather.

The relationship between the process of social change, which it is one function of the novel to articulate, and Fitzgerald's efforts to discover "some acceptable form" of moralizing is well illustrated in the two liaisons sustained by Anthony Patch in *The Beautiful and Damned*. The first of these, predating Anthony's marriage to Gloria, is with Geraldine Burke, an usher at Keith's motion-picture theater. The other is with Dot Raycroft, whom he meets when separated from Gloria by the war at an army camp in South Carolina.

Geraldine is an "amusement" for Anthony. He describes her to his friend Maury as having two "stunts": blowing her disordered hair out of her eyes, and saying "you cra-a-azy!" of anything beyond her limited comprehension. She ministers to Anthony's sense of superiority by her very being and, of course, to his pleasure as the gentleman's stereotypical casual sex object. Characteristically, Fitzgerald is terribly reticent about sex, and though Geraldine represents Anthony's liberation from conventional middle-class attitudes toward sex, the only manifestation of this liberation is an occasional exchange of "fairylike kisses" between the two. As a matter of fact, Fitzgerald's attitude toward sex is curiously ambivalent, as revealed in the story Anthony tells Geraldine of the gallant Chevalier O'Keefe, whose amatory successes cause him to retire to a monastery to be free from sex. O'Keefe tumbles to his death—and "eternal damnation"!—by plunging from a fanciful, monkish Tower of Chastity while trying to observe a peasant girl adjusting her garter. Attempting to celebrate the cavalier libertine, Fitzgerald is haunted by middle-class puritanism. However, despite Fitzgerald's uncertainty and reticence, Geraldine's role is clear. And she accepts it dutifully, recognizing that the usher at Keith's has no claims upon the gentleman.

The story of Dot Raycroft is a somewhat different one, despite the fact that she is evidently intended to fill a role similar to Geraldine's, as gentleman's sex object. However, by the time Anthony meets Dot he has already tumbled from his privileged position. No gentleman-soldier in the cavalier tradition, he is a mere private in a citizen army of draftees. And Dot is not so much an amusement as a comfort. So he sentimentalizes her, rather than condescend to her as he did with Geraldine. And he lives secretly with her for a time while he is in the army. But, of course, there are limits to even a declassed gentleman's needs. When the war is over, Anthony returns to Gloria, abandoning Dot in her southern rooming house. Naturally, like Geraldine, she should know her place. But she doesn't. Anthony declassed is closer to her than he was to Geraldine, more accessible however remote in New York. She loves him as Geraldine could not hope to. "Appallingly in earnest," she follows him to New York and begs to be taken back. Her very presence, her claim upon him, is of course a revelation of his diminished status. And he behaves appropriately, wrecking the apartment in an ungentlemanly effort to kill her.

The chaos he produces in his rage mirrors the disorder in society and in himself. And the stroke he suffers in consequence reduces him to a grotesque image of his deceased grandfather, whose wealth he now, ironically, inherits.

Throughout *The Beautiful and Damned* we observe Anthony Patch, the dilettante, unwilling and unable to work, self-indulgent, living a superficial life trivialized by the pursuit of petty pleasures. His life is the antithesis of that of old Adam Patch, who has made a fortune by energetic application and who devotes his declining years to castigating the unregenerate. At the end of the book we realize, however, that old Adam and his grandson are but two faces of a single coin. The image is an exact one, in fact, for both are creatures of a material, money-centered society. Empty of real values, both are given to proclaiming their whims as gospel. They are complementary versions of a decadent capitalist economy and an individualist ethic.

All too evidently the qualities they embody pervade the world of *The Beautiful and Damned*. In such a society the artist is a worthless parasite like Anthony's friend Richard Caramel, purveyor of sticky-sweet romances, trash for the movies through which he makes a fortune. In short, he is the sort of writer Fitzgerald rightly feared he was in danger of becoming by writing for money.

The man of mind in such a society is at best a conveyer of sardonic paradoxes, at worst a cynical exploiter of them. And along the way, in his cynicism and disgust, the intellectual may anticipate, as Maury Noble does, the simplistic fascist alternative to a chaos he perceives and fears. Here is Maury Noble reflecting on Nature:

> She had invented ways to rid the race of the inferior and thus give the remainder strength to fill her higher—or, let us say, her more amusing—

though still unconscious and accidental intentions. And actuated by the highest gifts of the enlightenment, we were seeking to circumvent her. In this republic I saw the black beginning to mingle with the white—in Europe there was taking place an economic catastrophe to save three or four diseased and wretchedly governed races from the one mastery that might organize them for material prosperity.

Thus Maury Noble. Noble indeed! One reflects with Ophelia, "O, what a noble mind is here o'erthrown!"

And what of the woman in this world from which all human values have been drained: Gloria. What of Gloria? Well, she is beautiful. And cold. When she is first introduced to Anthony, coming into his apartment on a frigid autumn day, she announces, "I'm a solid block of ice." The description is apt not merely because it gives her physical condition after coming in from a windy late November walk on Fifty-second Street. It describes her psychic condition as well. She is an icy goddess, a snow queen, frozen inside her own perfect white skin, completely self-regarding.

She talks about that skin, as Maury Noble observes early in the novel, "—her own skin. Always her own." As a matter of fact, everything is hers, by preemptive right. Anthony reflects, soon after meeting her, ". . . she took all the things of life for hers to choose from and apportion, as though she were continually picking out presents for herself from an inexhaustible counter."

All the *things* of life. The characteristic preoccupation of a material-centered society. And the preoccupation is chilling. Indeed, the whole ambience of the first third of the novel is an icy one. And of course Gloria shares that ambience. At twenty-two she has withdrawn from the game of life, the countless parties, the host of suitors. "He who fell in love with her now was dismissed utterly. . . . She went listlessly with the most indifferent men. She continually broke engagements, not as in the past from a cool assurance that she was irreproachable but indifferently. . . . She rarely stormed at men anymore—she yawned at them. She seemed . . . to her mother to be growing cold."

Of course the conventions of romance require that the handsome young prince thaw the snow queen. And he does. The first time Anthony kisses Gloria the winter night "was alive with thaw; it was so nearly warm that a breeze drifting low along the sidewalk brought to Anthony a vision of an unhoped-for hyacinthine spring." And taking her to a lower-class cabaret, filled with "credulous, sentimental, underpaid, overworked people," he sees her come alive. When he asks her if she objects to the place, she responds, " 'I love it. . . . I belong here,' she murmured, 'I'm like these people.' " And when Anthony from the height of his snobbish class consciousness objects, calling her a "young idiot," she insists: "No, I'm not. I *am* like them. . . . You ought to see. . . . You don't know me."

She is, in a sense, right. Anthony knows neither Gloria nor himself. The "streak of cheapness," the admiration for "gaudy vulgarity," that she sees in herself and reveals in, for example, her relationship with Bloeckman, actually characterize both her world and Anthony's. It is a world filled with trivial pleasures and gaudy baubles, a society whose only bond is the cash nexus.

She is right, too, when referring to the "credulous, sentimental, underpaid, overworked" people in the cabaret, she says, "I seem to belong here. These people could appreciate me and take me for granted, and these men would fall in love with me and admire me. . . ." Significantly enough, she is apotheosized for Anthony in this moment. "Anthony for the moment wanted fiercely to paint her, to set her down *now*, as she was, as, as with each relentless second she could never be again."

And he is also right. Gloria will never be thus again. For her identification with the lively vulgarity of the cabaret is the momentary identification of the onlooker, vicariously experiencing a life from which she herself is effectively shut off.

She is shut off by her fear of reality, her reiterated desire to be "safe." She is shut off by being an object with which her parents can bargain for a wealthy husband. She is shut off by her more or less charming childishness—chewing gumdrops, acting with selfish irresponsibility. Indeed one of the most touching and pathetic scenes in the book occurs after her marriage to Anthony, when he leaves her briefly to complete some minor task prior to their departure on the next leg of their wedding trip. Returning to their hotel room, he finds her asleep, clutching one of his old shoes to her tear-stained face as an infant would clutch its security blanket. The shoe is neither the glass slipper of Cinderella's extravagant but realized hope, nor one of the seven-league boots of world-bestriding youth, but the emblem of Gloria's childish isolation from the reality of life and the sign of her would-be prince's impotence.

For Anthony, too, is beset by fear, as is revealed on his wedding eve, when he is "upset and shaken" by the intrusion of coarse life, in the guise of an unknown woman's laughter, into the precious elegance of his bachelor apartment. And though he does thaw Gloria, the frigid snow queen, with a kiss and win her hand in marriage, he never succeeds in bringing her fully alive. In fact, the first episode in the book following Gloria and Anthony's wedding, although it is labelled "Con Amore," is concerned with the passing of love. And one of the first discoveries that Gloria makes as a wife is that Anthony is afraid. Significantly enough, the revelation comes in their hotel bedroom, amidst snickering bellboys and knowing night clerks, while Gloria hides in shame beneath the bedclothes and Anthony protests, in the manner of inadequate spouses, his "nervousness."

Beneath all the concern with pleasure then, with having a good time and not giving a damn, there is a considerable element of fear in the book. It surfaces most strikingly in the episode involving Joe Hull, a cheerful and ominous stranger with a yellow beard sprouting through his skin whom Maury Noble and Dick Caramel bring to the Patches' for an evening's carousing. Even Anthony is suspicious of him at first. However, his anxiety is soon drowned in alcohol, and only Gloria recognizes in Hull a dreadful embodiment of the destructive potential of their lives. When he attempts to fondle her, she struggles with him, and striking him, wrenches free, injuring her shoulder in the tussle, amidst a scene of drunken disorder. Later he reappears, a menacing terror outside her bedroom door, and she flees into the night, facing death by a speeding train in order to escape him.

The climactic debauch which loses for Gloria and Anthony old Adam Patch's inheritance, when he unexpectedly interrupts their revels, is less disconcerting than Gloria's flight from Joe Hull because it is too obviously staged, too carefully and melodramatically arranged. Nonetheless, its import is similar as Gloria and Anthony's awakening indicates:

> Then, on the August morning after Adam Patch's
> unexpected call, they awoke, nauseated and tired,

dispirited with life, capable only of one pervasive emotion—fear.

Fear. It is, in fact, the pervasive emotion in the book—fear of growing old, fear of sex, fear of work, fear of change, fear of life itself. And if insulation from it finally comes, with the story-book final inheritance of the pot of gold, it comes at such a cost with so mad a sacrifice of all human values as to transfer that fear from characters to readers. Anthony loses his humanity with his fear. He becomes a wealthy object. Our fear as readers is that such things can happen, that life can be so cruel, that the promise of youth can be utterly destroyed. We are appalled at the fact that amidst all the change we have observed in a world in flux, nothing has really changed. Anthony at the end of the book is much like his grandfather at its beginning. The wheel has come right round. The circle is closed. There is no place to go.

4

The Great *Gatsby*

The Beautiful and Damned was serialized in *The Metropolitan Magazine*, prior to its publication in book form, under an arrangement permitting the magazine's editor to make cuts in the manuscript. And cuts were made, cuts so serious as to vitiate the intended irony of the book's conclusion. When this fact was pointed out to Fitzgerald, who had needed the seven thousand dollars earned by the serialization to help pay for his and Zelda's disappointing trip to Europe, he commented sheepishly, "Well, they bought the rights to do anything they liked with it when they paid for it."

By the time the book was published, in April 1922, Fitzgerald had received $5,643 in advances from Scribner's. Shortly after publication of *The Beautiful and Damned*, Fitzgerald started digging his old magazine stories out of the files to make a book for "those who," as he said, "read as they run and run as they read." This collection, *Tales of the Jazz Age,* was like its predecessor *Flappers and Philosophers* (1921), put together with little concern for quality in an obvious effort to "cash in" on the popularity of the novel which preceded it.

When Fitzgerald turned to the theater, as he did in 1922 with a play called *The Vegetable,* his motive was profit. Speaking of his "awfully funny play," he says in a letter to Maxwell Perkins, it's "going to make me rich forever. It really is. I'm so damned tired of the feeling that I'm living up to my income." Of course, *The Vegetable* did not make him rich forever. On the contrary, when it finally reached production it failed dismally on its trial run in Atlantic City in the fall of 1923 and had to be abandoned.

Meanwhile, the Fitzgeralds had been moving about and spending money freely. There had been the trip to Europe. Then a visit to Montgomery, Alabama, with the thought of settling close to Zelda's parents until the baby was born. But Montgomery proved impossible, so they went to Fitzgerald's boyhood home in St. Paul, Minnesota. In 1921 Fitzgerald wrote to Perkins, reflecting on the chaos of his life:

> I'm having a hell of a time because I've loafed for 5 months and I want to get to work . . . . My 3rd novel, if I ever write another, will I am sure be black as death with gloom. I should like to sit down with ½ a dozen chosen companions and drink myself to death but I am sick alike of life, liquor and literature. If it wasn't for Zelda I think I'd disappear out of sight for three years. Ship as a sailor or something and get hard—I'm sick of the flabby semi-intellectual softness in which I flounder with my generation.

Thoughts of a new novel were evidently stirring. And

with them, feelings of guilt emerge, and the moralist begins to take over from the hedonist. Significantly Zelda is central in his thinking here. She is Fitzgerald's tie with reality, both a stay against despair when he is sick of life, liquor, and literature and an alternative to romantic hero mongering when he'd like to run off and be a sailor rather than settle down to work. But the new novel doesn't get written—not yet. For there is the play that is going to make him rich forever. And, after the birth of Scottie, a move back to New York that is going to require riches—thirty-six thousand dollars during the first year at Great Neck, where the Fitzgeralds settled into a three-hundred-dollar-a-month house with three servants and a Rolls-Royce.

To be sure, the Rolls was second hand. But the parties were original. And frequent. And expensive. The Rolls plied back and forth between Great Neck and New York's theaters, restaurants, cafés, and hotels with costly regularity. There were clothes and liquor. Food and liquor. House guests who stayed for weeks on end. And liquor. Despite the sale of the motion-picture rights to *This Side of Paradise* for ten thousand dollars, Fitzgerald was soon in debt again. So the novel that was to become *The Great Gatsby* was put aside while Fitzgerald ground out stories for the popular magazines—eleven in six months, for which he earned more than seventeen thousand dollars. But it took him six months to recuperate from the strain and he was "far from satisfied with the whole affair." Reflecting on the experience later in a letter to Edmund Wilson, he said, "I have got my health back—I no longer cough and itch and roll from one side of the bed to the other all night and have a hollow ache in my stomach after two cups of black coffee. I really worked hard as hell last winter—but it was all trash and it nearly broke my heart as well as my iron constitution."

Actually recovery was far less complete than Fitzgerald's letter to Wilson implies. Insomnia persisted. The pattern of work under extreme pressure followed by alcoholic release was set, and liquor, long an indulgence, became a dependence. Serious work was difficult to return to, and Fitzgerald began to detect in himself signs of the emotional bankruptcy that was evident in Ring Lardner, whom he got to know well in Great Neck where they were neighbors and drinking companions. In fact, Fitzgerald made heroic efforts to get Lardner to take himself seriously as a writer. He wanted Lardner to strengthen his reputation as an artist by gathering together his uncollected stories under the imprint of his own publisher, the distinguished literary firm of Charles Scribner's Sons. Fitzgerald's efforts, which finally culminated in Lardner's *How to Write Short Stories,* were doubtless occasioned not only by his respect for the talent of the writer and the dignity of the man. Fundamentally his attempts to spur Lardner to renewed work were the result of his recognition of an identity that they shared, an identity based on their shared fear that they were hollow within and on their attempts to escape from this fear through alcohol.

There were other problems, too, problems that might be summarized in a name: Zelda. Not that Zelda was alone responsible for the difficulties that arose. On the contrary, Fitzgerald himself was evidently more culpable. It was he who was becoming the problem drinker. It was he whose friable nerves gave under the tensions of conflicting aims of artistic and material success, of excessive work and dissatisfaction with its results. But he felt that he was working for Zelda and that she failed to appreciate either the effort expended or the waste of spirit that his commercially successful stories required. He accused her of indifference. He attacked her for prodigality. He belittled her intelligence. And Zelda, never one to take criticism lightly, responded in kind. He was parsimonious. Weak. An egotist. And he lacked talent.

Inevitably quarrels ensued. They were made up. But they became more frequent. Battles were followed by binges. To be followed by battles yet more fierce. And, of course, there were Fitzgerald's long hours of work, while Zelda fretted with nothing to do. Ring Lardner was a help, since he playfully courted Zelda, keeping her happy. But he kept Fitzgerald up through the night, drinking and discussing their common craft, in which Zelda had no part. There were, of course, the distractions of parties, guests, prodigal times, but as the relationship between Fitzgerald and Zelda became more strained, these became burdensome in their regularity, and in the demands they made on time, energy, and financial resources. Finally, in May 1924, the Fitzgeralds decided to break the pattern. They would try Europe again. Only this time not as tourists seeking to expand their horizons through travel. They would leave their old selves behind, and escaping the pattern that those selves had imposed upon experience, they would settle down upon the then unfrequented Riviera and find a new rhythm for their lives.

St-Raphaël was where they settled. But the new order they sought for their lives was interrupted by a discordant note: Zelda and a French aviator by the name of Edouard Jozan fell in love. It was a brief affair, unconsummated according to Jozan's later recollection. But Gerald and Sara Murphy, the leaders of the little group of American expatriates on the Riviera in those years, recalled that Zelda attempted suicide after Fitzgerald refused her a divorce and

insisted that the affair be broken off. It was broken off.
Jozan left. Recalling the episode later in *Save Me the
Waltz*, where Jozan appears under the name Jacques
Chevre-Feuille, Zelda says: "Whatever it was that she
wanted from Jacques, Jacques took it with him. . . . You
took what you wanted from life, if you could get it, and
you did without the rest."

"You took what you wanted from life, if you could get
it"—that was the code by which the Fitzgeralds had lived,
always believing that you could get whatever it was you
wanted. Now they had learned otherwise. Zelda had been of
central importance in Fitzgerald's life—the golden girl
whom he had won despite the odds, the woman by whom
he measured his success, at once the index and the substance of his reality. She had made—had been—his dream
come true. Now it failed. "That September 1924," he
commented later, "I knew something had happened that
could never be repaired." Now he must learn to live in that
broken world. And in a sense he did. Writing to Max Perkins as the terrible summer in France ended, he said: "It's
been a fair summer. I've been unhappy but my work hasn't
suffered from it. I am grown at last."

Measured by *The Great Gatsby*, that growth is certain. Infinitely superior to his earlier novels, it is by almost
any standard a nearly perfect book, one of the few permanent contributions to American literature to come out of an
epoch of great experimentation and high productivity.

Narrated by Nick Carraway, a young man of good
family and high ideals from the Midwest who has come
East to work in New York City, the novel focuses on Jay
Gatsby, who has risen from obscure beginnings as James
Gatz, a poor boy and a drifter, to great wealth, driven by a

dream resulting from his meeting and falling in love with a beautiful, rich girl whom he encounters by chance before leaving, as a soldier, for World War I.

Gatsby's dream might be described as the American dream of success. It is the dream of rising from rags to riches, of amassing a great fortune that will assure a life of luxuriant ease, power, and beauty in an ideal world untroubled by care and devoted to the enjoyment of everlasting pleasure with nothing to intervene between wish and fulfillment. It is a naive dream based on the fallacious assumption that material possessions are synonymous with happiness, harmony, and beauty. The dreamer overlooks or is unaware of the fact that the fullest kinds of pleasure come from the cultivation of sensibilities, the development of understanding, and the refinement of taste—accomplishments that have little to do with the acquisitive powers by which a fortune is amassed. Indeed, it is generally the case that the man who devotes all his energy to making money is deficient in those very qualities that make the life toward which he aspires desirable. The nouveaux riches, too newly rich to have had the leisure for self-cultivation, are frequently vulgar displayers of their new-won material possessions, lacking in culture, sophistication, and refinement.

Gatsby is such a man, a man who equates quantity with quality, cost with value. He lives in a tremendous mansion, tastelessly crammed with all the appurtenances of culture heterogeneously heaped together. He dresses in expensive bad taste. He gives parties for strangers costing fortunes, not having the time or the desire to make friends. He has an extensive library, elaborately housed, but no knowledge of books. The volumes on his shelves might as well be simply book jackets, since they are assembled as indices of his wealth, not for any pleasure or instruction they might provide him.

However, if Gatsby lacks culture and sophistication, he has a heart of gold. He has lived not for himself but for his dream, for his vision of the good life inspired by the beauty of a lovely rich girl. Hence he is open and unspoiled by what he has acquired. He is generous and, having lived with such intensity for the dream he has cherished, untouched by the moral evil that surrounds him. The fact of the matter is that he has made his money as a racketeer and consorts with unsavory characters or with parasites who accept his generosity with indifference, condescension, or contempt, and spread ugly rumors about the sources of his wealth. The established members of upper-class society see him as a clownish arriviste, crudely aping their ways.

The girl who has inspired Gatsby is Daisy Buchanan, whose beauty invested the wealthy background into which she was born with an air of mystery and charm for him. She has had a brief affair with Gatsby during the war. However, her parents deem him an unsuitable match for their daughter and prevent her from running off with him. Ultimately she marries Tom Buchanan, a crassly brutal egotist of vast inherited wealth whose insensitivity to moral and ethical values she, in fact, shares. He is unfaithful to her, but she covers up his lapses for him in the interest of preserving a facade of social respectability.

Action in the novel alternates between two wealthy Long Island communities—East Egg, bastion of traditional wealth, where the Buchanans reside; and West Egg, ostentatious showcase of the newly rich, where Gatsby displays his wealth in an effort to win Daisy back by demonstrating that he has arrived at her social level.

Beyond the rich Long Island Eggs lies the Valley of Ashes, a lower-middle-class Waste Land where people live out their drab lives as shopkeepers, garage mechanics, and servants of the rich in an atmosphere of bleak sterility. The neighborhood is dominated by a huge pair of sightless, staring eyes behind enormous spectacles, advertisement for Dr. T. J. Eckleburg, optometrist, and symbol of the indifference of a society characterized by lack of vision. Here Daisy and her husband display their indifference to human values in episodes involving sexual exploitation and careless violence. The principal victims of their moral indifference are Wilson, an automobile mechanic, and his wife Myrtle, who has become Tom Buchanan's mistress. Ultimately Gatsby falls victim to the train of violence their careless behavior sets off; he is shot down by Wilson, who mistakenly believes that Gatsby, rather than Daisy who has actually done it, has killed his wife. Daisy remains with Tom, indifferent to Gatsby's death as she had been to Myrtle's. It remains to Nick Carraway, the narrator, to register the human loss and measure the disparity between Gatsby's dream and the reality upon which it was based.

Even the minor details of the novel are handled with absolute sureness, Fitzgerald having learned to curb his penchant for making phrases for their own sake. Thus when early in the book he resorts to alliteration, telling us about the books on Nick Carraway's shelf "in red and gold like new money from the mint, promising to unfold the shiny secrets that only Midas and Morgan and Maecenas knew," the linguistic excess is not self-indulgence, as it almost certainly would have been in the earlier novels. It is, rather, an ironic device for placing the limited aspirations of Carraway as a novice bond salesman. When Carraway describes himself as having been "rather literary" in college, Fitzgerald doesn't use this, as he had done before, as an excuse for displaying his own jejune collegiate efforts. Instead we discover that the narrator had written "a series of very solemn and obvious editorials for the *Yale News.*" And when Carraway says that he is going to "become again that most limited of all specialists, the 'well-rounded man,'" Fitzgerald has him, modestly, defuse the phrase. "This isn't just an epigram—" he comments, "life is much more successfully looked at from a single window, after all."

Even the set passages where Fitzgerald is obviously "writing," are carefully controlled and integrated into the dramatic structure of the book. Take Gatsby's habadashery display. Along with the Marie Antoinette music rooms and Restoration salons, the period bedrooms "swathed in rose and lavender silk," the gardens and the "celebrated people" whom he assembles, his shirts are part of this West Egg Trimalchio's demonstration of his worth, by which he hopes to impress Daisy and win her back. Approaching his wardrobes, on an introductory tour of his pretentious mansion, Gatsby takes out a pile of shirts and begins throwing down on a table before Daisy and Nick

> shirts of sheer linen and thick silk and fine flannel,
> which lost their folds as they fell and covered the
> table in many-colored disarray. While we admired
> he brought more and the soft rich heap mounted
> higher—shirts with stripes and scrolls and plaids
> in coral and apple-green and lavender and faint
> orange, with monograms of Indian blue.

Touched by the intimate vulgarity of this display and recognizing that it is Gatsby's way of saying, "Look, I have arrived at your level of affluence and I love you," Daisy bends her head upon the shirts in an ecstasy of sobbing. The response has been criticized, by Milton Stern among others, who sees it as Fitzgerald's response, not Daisy's. "She should not," says Stern, "be seen as capable of ever deeply being one with Gatsby's dream." * But of course she is not so seen. What the scene reveals is that she has her vulgar side, a point reinforced by her response to the tasteless silver screen tableau of the director kissing his star at the party in Gatsby's garden. "I like her," Daisy says. "I think she's lovely." (One recalls Gloria's response to the cheap cabaret in *The Beautiful and Damned:* "I love it. . . . I belong here. . . . I'm like these people.")

Of course, Daisy does not "belong." As a denizen of East Egg, she is appalled by the raw crudeness of West Egg, which lacks the manners and restraint of the older society she knows and feels safe in. She doesn't like Gatsby's party, as he recognizes. It frightens her in its open indulgence of wild and erratic behavior. And when Daisy leaves the party early, we are shown how remote she is—in her preoccupation with manners, facades, pretenses—from being able to share the terrible simplicity of Gatsby's dream by her rejection of his milieu. Daisy, we are told, "saw something awful in the very simplicity she failed to understand."

Moreover, it should be pointed out that the scene of Daisy's tears over Gatsby's shirts is not an isolated episode but is structurally parallel to another scene in which Daisy "cried and cried." The scene is the one recalled by Jordan Baker, an old friend of Daisy's with whom Nick Carraway almost falls in love. In that scene, preceding Daisy's marriage to Tom, Daisy has drunk herself into a state of maudlin self-pity, and she weeps not over a pile of shirts but over the $350,000 string of pearls with which Tom Buchanan has, in effect, bought her. The necklace is Tom's wedding gift to her, and drunk, she can reject him and the

* Milton Stern: *The Golden Moment: The Novels of F. Scott Fitzgerald.* New York: Holt, Rinehart and Winston, 1965.

power his wealth represents. Temporarily she does so, throwing the pearls into a wastebasket. But she is quickly sobered up by Jordan Baker and hustled down to her bridal dinner. And her tears of anger and outrage and despair are as quickly forgotten as later her tears of joy and remorse for joy lost will be. She forgets Gatsby as quickly as she comes to accept Tom Buchanan. More quickly. For the comic grotesque scene of her drunken rejection of Tom requires the assistance of Jordan Baker, spirits of ammonia, and a cold bath before she can face her bridal dinner. The anti-communion that ends the Gatsby affair—cold fried chicken and two bottles of ale shared in the Buchanan kitchen—requires no preparation to reestablish an "air of natural intimacy" between Tom and Daisy. And, of course, Gatsby takes the grotesque and final cold bath, when he is shot to death in his own swimming pool by Wilson.

Thus even seemingly minor details reverberate widely in the novel. Hence a nameless little man with enormous "owl-eyed spectacles," in a marvelously comic scene in Gatsby's pretentious Gothic library, has the natural keenness of vision to penetrate both Gatsby's persona and the common conception of what lies behind it and to recognize the thoroughness with which Gatsby has filled out his "Platonic conception of himself." Owl-eyes takes a book from one of the shelves in the library—a demonstration, like all he surrounds himself with, of Gatsby's "worth"—and exclaims triumphantly, having anticipated fake books:

> "See! . . . It's a bona-fide piece of printed matter. It fooled me. This fella's a regular Belasco. It's a triumph. What thoroughness! What realism! Knew when to stop, too—didn't cut the pages."

The passage, down to the uncut pages, is a gem. And it is rich in multiple ironies, with natural vision being

focused through thick glasses to reveal the genuine beneath
the sham, the genuine in the sham. Moreover, it is the
nameless individual imaged in the predatory night bird
who not only sees through the newly rich racketeer to the
person beneath (a man who is a man because he is, first,
a visionary, a fact that the owl-eyed one does not see), but
also is himself the sole man in the host of names who have
attended Gatsby's parties. It is he alone (along with Nick
Carraway) who returns to Gatsby's funeral in the rain to
say a mocking "Amen" to the minister's ritualistic "Blessed
are the dead that the rain falls on" and to deliver the real
invocation himself through his coarse worldly assessment:
"The poor son-of-a-bitch."

Associated with Nick Carraway, the narrator who
"sees" the events of the story for us, Owl-eyes in his brief
appearances helps to register Gatsby's true worth in terms of
a complex irony. But Fitzgerald does more with him. His
owlish glasses are reflected in the enormous spectacles of
Dr. T. J. Eckleburg, which look out, symbolically, over the
valley of ashes between West Egg and New York City.
A magnified advertising image of that keen vision that enables Owl-eyes to place Gatsby, these gigantic spectacles
dominate the waste land beyond the rich Eggs. But, of
course, there is no seeing in them. And the waste land,
though revealed, remains, paradoxically, unseen. Moreover,
the magnified image takes on ominous meaning by virtue
of the very absence of the quality that Owl-eyes possesses.
Dr. Eckleburg's glasses are the visual counterpart of Wallace Stevens' listener, in "The Snow Man,"

> . . . who listens in the snow,
> And, nothing himself, beholds
> Nothing that is not there and the nothing that is.

To be sure, there are many beholders in *The Great*

Gatsby, which is a novel about seeing—about vision—as much as it is about anything. Perhaps the principal be-holder in the book is Nick Carraway, the narrator. And he is one of the principal reasons for its success, for he enables the author to step back from the story and tell it more clearly and completely than he could otherwise, without stumbling in the characters' shoes and betraying their voices with his own. Not that the experiences depicted in *Gatsby* are not in some ultimate interior emotional sense Fitz-gerald's own. They are, of course. He certainly saw himself as, like Gatsby, a Midwestern Mr. Nobody from Nowhere who dreamed his greatness and lived it true, overtopping in the process the casual possessors of power and assurance from the Eastern establishment. Like Gatsby, too, his dream was intertwined with the winning of a girl. But Fitzgerald had only *almost* lost Zelda, and fiction had to test the alternative. Other losses that the author had sus-tained—his failure to win Ginevra King, for example—could supply the emotional weight required by the story. But the single end of the fictional event, while it allowed Fitzgerald to use all his experiences, could not permit him to retread each several detour that life afforded without losing the significant shape that fiction demanded. The narrator helped him to preserve that shape by keeping the events that comprised it from becoming, in Gatsby's words, "just personal."

Moreover, Fitzgerald was not simply Gatsby, nor Gatsby altogether. Part of him was Nick Carraway, a sensi-tive if somewhat snobbish young man from the Midwest who could trace his family's rise to the none-too-scrupulous commercial ideals of his granduncle. If Gatsby is given to the dream of "the orgiastic future," to be achieved by what-ever means, Carraway's reserving of judgment and concern for the springs of action come from another side of Fitzgerald, a side rooted, like the first, in his family and early life.

This rootedness—in the family and in the Midwest—is an important aspect of Nick Carraway. It is evident from the very beginning of the novel, where we learn that Nick has come back "restless" from World War I, feeling that "instead of being the warm center of the world, the Middle West now seemed like the ragged edge of the universe." When he decides "to go East to learn the bond business," a family council is called to sanction—"Why—ye-es"—his going, financed by his father for a year. And, of course, right here at the start we learn that he did not stay. Before Gatsby's story begins, Nick says: "I came East, permanently, I thought, in the spring of twenty-two." So he thought. He will have second thoughts.

Of course, Nick Carraway's Midwest is more than simply a place. Recalling the act of returning from eastern prep school and college at Christmastime, Nick exclaims, "That's my Middle West—not the wheat or the prairies or the lost Swede towns, but the thrilling returning trains of my youth . . . ." It is a Middle West compounded of the chatter of frozen breath and hands waving overhead in greeting, of the matching of invitations in the Chicago railroad station, and of old acquaintances renewed in a spirit of holiday gaiety that transforms even the "murky yellow cars of the Chicago, Milwaukee & St. Paul railroad" and makes them look as "cheerful as Christmas itself." The very snow, the "real snow" beyond Chicago as the train moves west, is humanized. It is "our snow."

And so we move, in remembered time, from the hectic gaiety of Chicago to the homely warmth, amid the season's cold, of "street lamps and sleigh bells in the frosty dark and the shadows of holly wreaths thrown by lighted windows on the snow," in a city where "dwellings are still called through decades by a family's name." We move from the nameless "Miss This-or That's" finishing schools to the Ordways', the Herseys', and the Schultzes'. We move "through the cold vestibules" of moving trains to "the warm center of the world," "unutterably aware of our identity with this country for one strange hour, before we [melt] indistinguishably into it again."

This is Nick Carraway's sustaining memory, a homely memory of a growing boy's life articulated each step of the way into the life of a town in a natural and happy way, so that his values are rooted deep in communal life and experience. It is the counterpoint to Gatsby's sustaining dream, which it frames and interprets, a dream of aspiration that moves Gatsby to follow it to imagined glory and unforeseen defeat.

Gatsby's career, his "greatness," which is at once heroic and grotesque, is of course the center of the novel. That career, an archetype of the American business success story, begins, as so many heroic careers do, by chance, when young James Gatz happens to be drifting along the south shore of Lake Superior where Dan Cody's yacht drops anchor. On a whim, Dan picks him up and gives him his start. (Young Jimmy Gatz changes his name to Jay Gatsby at this point, signalizing the beginning of a new life.) And that is quite a start, for Cody is made in the image of the robber barons, those unscrupulous men who, in post-Civil War America, built empires in coal, oil, railroads, lumber, and various other enterprises. They did so by a combination of gambler's luck, driving ambition, unscrupulous exploitation, and unparalleled arrogance, with un-trammeled freedom, in the absence of laws to control them under the so-called free enterprise system, satiating their greed for wealth and power. In the process they harnessed America's natural resources, industrialized the country, and by accumulating vast reservoirs of capital, established an economic oligarchy that was to control the wealth of America down to our own times.

Jay Gatsby learns his business techniques from Dan Cody, rough-handed techniques that, in a later day when the self-made man on the make is subject to some control in the public interest, will be seen as the techniques of the gangster, racketeer, or outlaw. He also learns something of the crude rewards of such endeavors from Cody, "the pioneer debauchee, who during one phase of American life brought back to the Eastern seaboard the savage violence of the frontier brothel and saloon." Indeed, Gatsby feels the savagery of that way of life when, upon Cody's death, he is cheated out of the money the old man had left him by Cody's avaricious mistress, who is responsible for the old man's death and who uses the money she acquires through it to corrupt justice and take his entire fortune, including Gatsby's share.

Such is the reality of Jay Gatsby's preparation for his rise to fortune. But of course the reality of such a career is rarely faced. There is a myth to disguise the sordid truth and "explain" success. And Fitzgerald gives us that fable, too, running in ironic counterpoint to the reality. High purpose, stringent discipline, unremitting toil, good training, and high idealism comprise the myth. And so we have young James Gatz living according to a schedule, beginning with rising at 6 A.M. and leaving time for exercise, study, sport, and the practice of "elocution, poise and how to attain it" within the none-too-frequent gaps of an eight-hour work day. Dale Carnegie could have done no better. Nor could he have topped young Gatz's "General Resolves," copied into the flyleaf of a dime Western:

> No wasting time at Shafters or [a name indecipherable]
> No more smokeing or chewing.
> Bath every other day
> Read one improving book or magazine per week
> Save $5.00 [crossed out] $3.00 per week
> Be better to parents

Down to the spelling and the second thoughts, the list is a masterpiece, as complete in its way as the books with the uncut pages in the Gothic library are in theirs.

To be sure, preparation for a career is not the career itself. There is the romantic substance of that career. And, of course, Fitzgerald gives us the details of the young ruby-collecting, big-game hunting, dilettante painter, living "like a young rajah in all the capitals of Europe." Right out of Hollywood, with Douglas Fairbanks in the leading role. Only a phrase should be added to the traditional disclaimer —"Any resemblance to living characters, or *language*, is purely coincidental." Carraway has it just right when he describes Gatsby as "a turbaned 'character' leaking sawdust at every pore as he pursued a tiger through the Bois de Boulogne."

It is all there, the sordid or commonplace facts and the fantastic legend together. And paradoxically, Gatsby has lived both. He is a kind of circus character—the Great Gatsby! Yet he is great in another sense, too, having made the grandiose legend come true. He has the tiger skin. A chestful of medals pins down his seemingly extravagant claims about exploits in World War I. When his underworld companion, Meyer Wolfsheim, calls him "an Oggsfoid man," Gatsby has a picture taken in Trinity Quad with the Earl of Doncaster to prove that he did in fact go to Oxford, if only for five months. Now to be sure, five months at Oxford do not make an Oxford man, nor does a chestful of medals prove that a man is valorous any more than a vast estate on Long Island indicates that he has arrived socially. But Gatsby, with naive innocence, believes they do. And what is ultimately important is not that he has gained these symbols of accomplishment—the medals, the picture, the house, are shoddy enough demonstrations of worth. What is important is Gatsby's belief, his dream.

It is Gatsby's dream that establishes the ultimate congruence of fancy and fact. For the dream is held with a passionate intensity that transforms fact. The dream is of course of Daisy, who represents for Gatsby the ultimate possibility of accomplishment and fulfillment. She is Gatsby's "Belle Dame sans Merci." An ambivalent figure, she is like John Keats's "Belle Dame," who, representing the shaping power of the imagination, is more real than the kings and princes, the men of power, who fade to pale ghosts when juxtaposed beside her. But La Belle Dame's lover fades, too, waking from his dream of fulfillment to find he has dreamed,

> The latest dream I ever dream'd
> On the cold hill's side.

And Keats concludes,

> And this is why I sojourn here,
> Alone and palely loitering,

Though the sedge is wither'd from the lake,
  And no birds sing.

Reflecting on Gatsby's end, Nick says:

> . . . he must have felt that he had lost the old
> warm world, paid a high price for living too long
> with a single dream. He must have looked up at
> an unfamiliar sky through frightening leaves and
> shivered as he found what a grotesque thing a rose
> is and how raw sunlight was upon the scarcely
> created grass. A new world, material without being
> real, where poor ghosts, breathing dreams like air,
> drifted fortuitously about . . . like that ashen, fan-
> tastic figure gliding toward him through the amor-
> phous trees.

The fantastic figure comes from the unimagined world
—"material without being real"—from the valley of ashes
beneath the blank spectacles of Dr. Eckleburg. He is, of
course, Wilson, a poor ghost whose dreams, unlike Gatsby's,
are "like air," substanceless, his world empty and meaningless. His wife Myrtle has not been an inspiration, like
Daisy, but a reminder of his own fortuitousness and of his
humiliation. Tom Buchanan has used her, crassly and
brutally, as his mistress. Daisy has killed her, by chance, in
a hit-and-run accident while driving Gatsby's car. When
Wilson, bewildered, seeks solace after her death, he turns to
the great sightless eyes of the optometrist's advertising sign,
an ironic surrogate for God in the visionless, material,
chance-dominated world he inhabits. Looking up at the
giant eyes in the sky outside the window of his auto repair
shop where Myrtle lies dead, he says, "God sees
everything."

A neighbor reminds him that "that's an advertisement." But the correction makes no impression on Wilson. How should it? He is an inhabitant of the "new world," dominated by the rich and unscrupulous who care nothing for human values Tom has patronized him. His wife's love has been bought with cheap gifts. Her violent death has been disregarded as a matter of no consequence. Such a world is a waste land, a land of dust and ashes in which God is dead and the inhabitants are mere ghosts.

Ashen and fantastic, Wilson mimics Gatsby's duality. A part of the "foul dust that floated in the wake" of Gatsby's dream, he is, in a sense, that dream itself, defeated and negated, as the valley of ashes is the collapsed shape of the gaudy Eggs. Naturally Wilson destroys Gatsby —and himself. For, of course, the "new world" extends beyond the bleak slumlike valley of ashes, which is but its ultimate symbol.

The orgiastic future that Gatsby dreams has its obverse in Nick Carraway's nightmare vision. Nick, who grew up in a house that had been called the Carraways' for decades and whose memory is saturated with a festive communal life redolent of Dickens, sees West Egg as a group of grotesque houses crouching beneath a lusterless moon. There four "men in dress suits are walking along the sidewalk with a stretcher on which lies a drunken woman in a white evening dress, her hand sparkling cold with jewels." In this sinister vision, "Gravely the men turn in at a house—the wrong house. But no one knows the woman's name, and no one cares." The nightmare fuses many elements: Gatsby's alcoholic parties with their indifferent guests; Daisy, drunk, with the pearls that have bought her, poured into her wedding dress for delivery to the wrong man; Myrtle laid out on the garage bench, her indifferent slayer driving on; Tom turning in at a jewelry store—rid forever of Nick's provincial squeamishness—to buy another pearl necklace and begin another affair.

No one cares. To be sure, in the radiance of Gatsby's single vision everyone is greeted as a familiar; "Old sport," he calls them all. But he has no friends. No one cares who gives the parties. Nobody goes to his funeral except Owl-eyes and Nick. "No one else was interested," as Nick says, "—interested, I mean, with that intense personal interest to which everyone has some vague right at the end." Rich as he was, he is a poor son-of-a-bitch like us all in the end. His dream belied his common humanity. He has been the Great Gatsby, a P. T. Barnum figure. His death gives him back his humanity. And if Nick is correct and Gatsby sees "a new world, material without being real" at the end with the loss of his dream, it gives him another kind of greatness, the greatness that comes with tragic insight.

In any case, Nick is certainly right when, on an impulse of the heart, he turns to Gatsby for the last time and shouts across the lawn as he leaves the estate: "They're a rotten crowd. . . . You're worth the whole damn bunch put together."

The rotten crowd includes not only the Whitebaits, the Hammerheads, and the Belugas; the Blackbucks, the Beavers, and the Civets; the Belchers, the Smirkes, and the Haags—fish, flesh, and foul from West Egg—but the Buchanans, the Sloans, and the Bakers, the East Egg crowd, as well. Actually, the two groups are as like as two eggs. In fact, the latter group is the worse of the two, for they pretend to a dignity and stability, to a moral authority, to which their behavior does not entitle them.

Tom Buchanan is the most obvious example of the

rottenness of the East Eggians. Calling himself a pessimist, he mouths racial clichés and displays his muddleheadedness—"It seems that pretty soon the earth's going to fall into the sun—or wait a minute—it's just the opposite—the sun's getting colder every year"—with imperfectly remembered, stale ideas out of "scientific" books, "deep books with long words in them" in Daisy's mocking description. Arrogant and brutal, he is a flagrant philanderer, a snob, a liar.

Nick sees Jordan Baker, early on in the book, as a "clean, hard, limited person, who dealt in universal skepticism." He recognizes her dishonesty in small matters and overlooks it, as he overlooks her avidity for gossip. (She listens in on private telephone conversations and knows—and tells Nick—the Daisy-Gatsby story.) In fact, beneath her cool, clean exterior, she is as limited as Myrtle's sister Catherine, who applauds Myrtle's liaison with Tom. "Tom's the first sweetie she ever had," Catherine says approvingly to Nick. Jordan, believing that Daisy should take Gatsby as a lover, says "Daisy ought to have something in her life." Nick comes to see through Jordan, recognizing in her jaunty carelessness a profound disregard for other people and the basis of her identity with Daisy and the corruption of East Egg.

In *The Great Gatsby* Daisy is, of course, the principal representative of that carelessness. In her the charming willfulness of Fitzgerald's self-indulgent hedonists takes on sinister implications. The scene that Jordan Baker gives us and, significantly, participates in, sobering Daisy up and nudging her into marriage with Tom as she nudged a golf ball closer to the hole on another occasion, is filled with images of that self-indulgent carelessness: a bottle of Sauterne, a wastebasket full of pearls, and lovely Daisy in her flowered dress, drunk and muttering, "Daisy's change' her mine. . . . Daisy's change' her mine!" The phrases indicate that she has changed her mind and will not marry Tom. But of course she changes her mind again, finding in the man who came down to Louisville from Chicago to marry her, with a hundred people in four private railroad cars, and with the string of pearls worth $350,000, a new "mine."

Daisy is, to say the least, inconstant. That she can carelessly change her "mine," or mind, unites Daisy with Tom, who changes his with equal carelessness and great frequency, finding in every chambermaid or chance acquaintance a new opportunity. Damaging to Daisy's self-esteem, Tom's casual fornications bind her to him as she collaborates in efforts to conceal his infidelities, caught rather than liberated by her self-regard.

And, of course, she catches others, making messes of their lives as she does of her own. A siren, she lures men with her throaty, mysterious voice, a voice containing the promise of infinite riches. But the minute her voice breaks off, Nick feels the "basic insincerity" of what she has just said. The infinite riches turn out to be—only money. "Her voice is full of money," Gatsby says, recognizing the reality that has informed his dream. For the book is about wealth and reality as much as it is about vision or dream. Alas, the dream fails, leaving Gatsby in a "new world, material without being real," a world in which he cannot live, for he lives by the dream.

Of course, no one can live by a dream altogether either, as the concluding paragraphs of the book make clear. There the green light at the end of Daisy's dock and the fresh green breast of the island that "flowered once for Dutch sailors' eyes" are conjoined as emblems of "the orgiastic future that year by year recedes before us"—Hendrick Hudson, Gatsby, Nick, you, I—all. Or all for whom a green vision panders in whispers to the greatest of all human dreams "for a transitory enchanted moment." Naturally the moment is transitory, whatever the voyage, quest, or struggle that brings us to it. And as we confront the about-to-be-realized goal, it is already behind us "somewhere back in the vast obscurity beyond the city, where the dark fields of the republic [roll] on under the night."

So the most carefully wrought and beautifully complete of Fitzgerald's books ends with a return to the dark fields of the republic from which all of its characters, like its author, came. For, as Nick says before returning to "the warm center of the world" from the "ragged edge of the universe," this has been "a story of the West, after all."

5

Love Battle

The Great Gatsby was published in April 1925. Looking back at that time years later in a letter to his daughter, Fitzgerald indicates what his course should have been, what he should have "said at the end of *The Great Gatsby*: 'I've found my line—from now on this comes first. This is my immediate duty—without this I am nothing.'" He was right, in a sense. He had found his line. But he failed to follow it. It was nine years before he published his next novel, *Tender Is the Night*. In the interval he plunged deep into the nothingness that he saw as the alternative to taking up his immediate duty. He describes that nothingness in *The Crack-Up*: "In the dead of night . . . I see the real horror develop over the roof-tops. . . . Horror and waste—Waste and horror—What I might have been and done that is lost, spent, gone, dissipated, unrecapturable. . . . The horror has come now like a storm." But he was wrong, too, in his retrospective analysis, for paradoxically, his nothing was to be his all. The waste and horror of his life were to be the subject of his greatest book, the book that he spent nine years to live and write.

"The horror has come now like a storm." As with most storms, there were mutterings, rumblings, and crashes of thunder long before it broke. We have heard some of those warnings. Perhaps the loudest crash was Zelda's brief affair with Edouard Jozan. That broke open the sky. It would close again, and halcyon days would follow on the Riviera and elsewhere. But the close and complex relationship between the writer and his wife, which had been strained from time to time before this, would never be quite the same hereafter.

Passionate, impulsive, strong-willed, and egocentric, Zelda had always resented the demands that Fitzgerald's art made upon him. For one thing, subordinating her to another interest, it took him away from her for hours, days, weeks at a time. For another, it interfered with the pursuit of pleasure to which they were both committed. In fact, Fitzgerald's dedication as a writer seemed to belie that other commitment, which he professed as strongly as she. Moreover, the artist's serious work put limits to the earning power by the promise of which he had won Zelda. And finally, his writing gave him a kind of cachet in which she could not share. This latter factor was an important one in a relationship where friendly rivalry was a significant element in most activities, as it was for the Fitzgeralds. As the relationship grew strained and tensions developed, the rivalry became less friendly and took on—for Zelda, at least —a quality of desperation.

How very desperate it was, Hemingway, who first got to know the Fitzgeralds in Paris in the spring of 1925, attests in *A Moveable Feast*. In that book, published in

1964, Hemingway professes to have known that Zelda was already mad when he first met her. And he suggests that she tried to destroy Fitzgerald, both as a writer and as a man. His claim is that she was jealous of Fitzgerald's work and attempted to divert him from the discipline of writing by encouraging his drinking and partying, and by her own wild and imprudent behavior. She also, if Hemingway can be believed, denigrated Fitzgerald's manhood with accusations of sexual inadequacy.

The difficulty is that Hemingway cannot be believed— at least, not altogether. His own feelings about Fitzgerald were deeply ambivalent. He respected Fitzgerald's talent but suspected his character and strength. He had the contempt of the "manly" man who could handle his liquor and satisfy his women for one who could do neither—and couldn't ski or box either! Moreover, he detested Zelda, who thought him "bogus." But Hemingway's picture of the Fitzgeralds in the Paris of the twenties, however highly colored and distorted by his own egotism, jealousy, and contempt, cannot be ignored. The terrible tensions were there, and from his own angle Hemingway saw and reported them.

Other witnesses corroborate Hemingway's picture of strained personal relations between the Fitzgeralds, a strain to which alcohol certainly contributed, though it is evident from Hemingway's own book that Fitzgerald needed no encouragement from Zelda in that direction. In fact, alcohol had by this time taken a firm hold upon him. There were week-long bouts of heavy drinking, after which Fitzgerald would awaken in unknown hotel rooms in strange cities, unaware of how he got there. There were serious manifestations of antisocial behavior, like Fitzgerald's brawl with a group of Roman taxidrivers. Fitzgerald was badly beaten and thrown into jail, from which Zelda rescued him on this occasion.

But the whole tenor of the Fitzgeralds' life changed during this period. They were older now, and the merry pranks of their youthful days in New York just after the First World War began to seem more than a little strained. Friends began to object to their eccentric behavior. Onlookers registered disdain or disgust, rather than the more satisfying sense of outrage. So the Fitzgeralds tried a little harder to be outrageous, vying with one another. Their escapades became cruder, tainted with viciousness. The air was heavy with threats, recriminations. Tears were frequent. Violence was never far off.

To be sure, there was the lovely summer of 1925—the "great time"—at Antibes on the French Riviera. And the summer following it at Juan-les-Pins. Long lazy days on the hot sand by the blue Mediterranean. And a congenial group of friends and fellow artists in a small colony surrounding the wealthy American expatriates Sara and Gerald Murphy. The Murphys had the happy faculty of making every day into a party and every guest feel himself to be the brilliant center of festivities. Fitzgerald was quickly drawn to them and observed them closely, writing them into the book he was working on. (They would contribute something of themselves to the characters of Nicole and Dick Diver in *Tender Is the Night*, as Ring Lardner, who visited the little colony, would contribute to that of Abe North.)

But the book—it was called, variously, *The World's Fair*, *The Boy Who Killed His Mother*, and *Our Type*— was far from finished when the Fitzgeralds returned to America, where Fitzgerald had an unsuccessful try at writing for the movies and continued to drink heavily.

Zelda, who had begun to paint seriously while in Europe, and would later try to compete with her husband as a writer, now took up dancing, studying ballet. She was almost twenty-eight! Yet she would have a career as a dancer. Fitzgerald saw the futility of it. And resented her intense concentration when his own powers were obviously failing. They fought with the savageness that intimate knowledge of the weaknesses and strengths of one's opponent makes possible. Then they isolated themselves from one another, pitting their wills against the problems of their separate disciplines and their own weaknesses. Coming together, bearing the burdens of their private defeats, they fought again, relentlessly.

So it went, as they drove themselves against one another and rushed away from the horrible encounters—to New York, Hollywood, Wilmington, Paris, Cannes, Wilmington, Paris, Algiers, Paris—in a crazy whirl. Fitzgerald drunk, bitter, frustrated in his work, vicious; Zelda strained, working tensely for a separate identity, not to be put down, lonely, vulnerable, and savage.

Finally, in April 1930, Zelda broke down. She was taken to a sanitorium in Montreux, Switzerland. Diagnosis: schizophrenia. Symptoms: terrible hallucinations and unbearable eczema. Duration: April 1930 to September 1931. Almost a year of torture, followed by gradual and seemingly complete recovery.

The Fitzgeralds returned to the United States and settled in Montgomery, near Zelda's parents. Fitzgerald went to Hollywood for his second unsuccessful try at writing for the movies. While he was away, Zelda's father died. And Zelda suffered a second breakdown.

Prospects for complete recovery were now, as Fitzgerald knew, extremely remote. However, even while she was hospitalized in Baltimore, Zelda, driven by her terrible will, completed a novel in six short weeks, the book that was published as *Save Me the Waltz*, after her husband and Maxwell Perkins, to whom she sent the manuscript, persuaded her to soften the attack that it contained on Fitzgerald. Nevertheless, though Zelda had lucid periods and was able to live with Fitzgerald for varying periods of time, intermittently free of institutions, she never recovered completely.

Facing the reality of his wife's condition, Fitzgerald looked for a house in Baltimore where he could be near Zelda and have her with him when that was possible. He found one at Rodgers Forge on the Bayard Turnbull estate, a large old Victorian house called La Paix. There he settled down to try to write himself out of debt, care for Scottie, nurse Zelda and watch for inevitably recurring signs of madness, and battle with his own alcoholism. All this while attempting to complete *Tender Is the Night* and reestablish his now faded literary reputation. Small wonder that, writing to Edmund Wilson from the house, he headed one of his letters "La Paix (My God!)."

There was little peace to be found in that house or in Fitzgerald's life during those years. Nor is it to be sought in the book upon which he was working. Though the idea of matricide, on which Fitzgerald had originally intended to base his novel, had been abandoned, there was in its place an incestuous rape, resulting in the madness that lies close to the heart of the book and shadows its every page. The story begins chronologically in 1917 in wartime Switzerland, "an island washed on one side by the waves of thunder around Gorizia and on another by the cataracts along the

Somme and the Aisne." In one episode a Russian aristocrat is aided in his escape from recently sovietized Russia, and three Red Guards are killed. One of the principal figures in the escape is a man whose violent life has necessitated an operation in which one eighth of his skull has been removed. In another episode the hero of the book is brutally beaten by irate Roman taxicab drivers and then thrown in jail, where he is stomped and clubbed, his nose and a rib broken and an eye almost gouged out. At his appearance in court he is mistaken by a crowd of angry spectators for the rapist-killer of a five-year-old child. There are two shootings, a duel, and two suicide attempts. A man is beaten to death, and a woman dies, exhausted by the intensity of her battle with excruciating pain. Even the firing of Nicole and Dick Diver's drunken cook is only accomplished after a gladiatorial combat involving a heavy cane with a bronze knob on it, a cleaver, and a butcher's knife.

Yet the book is not an adventure yarn. It is a love story, though a curious one. It is the story of Dick Diver, Dr. Richard Diver, an American psychiatrist, who marries his patient, Nicole Warren. She is a beautiful young rich girl suffering from a neurotic disorder that results from having been seduced by her father, Mr. Devereux Warren, "a fine American type" as the doctor in charge of the sanitorium where he tries to dump his problem daughter without explaining her problem ironically calls him. (Actually, Warren is a Chicago plutocrat with a thin veneer of worldliness and the gross sensibility of a peasant, an embodiment of the unscrupulousness of American money and power. This unscrupulousness, magnified by arrogance and masked by a somewhat thicker veneer of worldliness, is confirmed in his eldest daughter, "Baby" Warren, who rounds out Fitzgerald's picture of the American imperium.) Viewed partly through the eyes of Rosemary Hoyt, a young American movie star traveling in Europe with her mother, the early years of the Divers' marriage are seen as a series of idyllic days spent beside the Mediterranean under what can only be called the inspired direction of Dick. Dick creates a little paradise at Tarmes and sustains it by the power of his will and the pressure of his charm, a paradise threatened only by Nicole's periodic lapses toward insanity. But the effort is too much for him in the long run, and he begins to go to pieces as Nicole, cured by his devotion, returns to normalcy. The end of the idyll is signalized by Dick's delayed, abortive affair with Rosemary, and it is finally terminated when Nicole takes Tommy Barban, an intimate of the charmed circle at Tarmes, as her lover. Dick returns to America alone, to drift into obscurity as the novel ends.

Perhaps "love battle" describes the story better. That is the seemingly incongruous phrase Dick uses to describe the bloody Second Battle of the Marne when he takes his wife and some friends out to examine the battlefield site at the beginning of the third book of the novel. He says—and his words are, I believe, an important index to the several levels of meaning that the novel expresses—"Why, this was a love battle—there was a century of middle-class love spent here. This was the last love battle." Diver is, of course, speaking of the passionate fervor with which the World War I battle was fought, as well as of the fact that it was fought between intimates, practically—members of the same class, neighbors in the European community; people with the same backgrounds, feelings, memories, and expectations; people as close to one another as lovers.

Dick's intention becomes clearer as he describes the terrible intensity and dogged determination with which the battle was fought. Pointing to the little stream in the near distance that he and his companions could walk to in two minutes, he says, "It took the British a month to walk to it—a whole empire walking very slowly, dying in front and pushing forward behind. And another empire walked very slowly backward a few inches a day, leaving the dead like a million bloody rugs." Measuring the progress of the holocaust in the slow footsteps of an afternoon walk and its consequences in a horrifying image of domestic luxury, Diver unites on the scale of inches the fate of empire and the atmosphere of middle-class parlors. This intimate European bonding of duty and feeling, this destructive locking together of personal preoccupations and public issues, "took religion and years of plenty and tremendous sureties and the exact relation that existed between the classes." To have participated in it, "you had to have a whole-souled sentimental equipment going back further than you could remember."

Clearly Dick Diver has this "whole-souled sentimental equipment." Dick's father, patterned on Fitzgerald's own, has transmitted it to the boy, saving him from a spoiling, after his wife loses her first two children, by becoming his son's moral guide and raising him to believe that nothing can be "superior to 'good instincts,' honor, courtesy, and courage." These old-fashioned virtues go back to the Divers, Dorseys, and Hunters in the Virginia cemetery where Dick, with appropriate piety, buries his father "amid the souls . . . of the seventeenth century," bidding, "Good-by, my father—good-by, all my fathers."

Moreover, Dick has fallen in love with Nicole, a mental patient, despite the advice of his friend and professional colleague and his own professional knowledge of the dangers such a relationship will entail. Surely this is a sentimental response.

And he nourishes "illusions of eternal strength and health, and of the essential goodness of people. . . ." These illusions, particularly the latter, Fitzgerald describes as "illusions of a nation, the lies of generations of frontier mothers who had to croon falsely, that there were no wolves outside the cabin door." Again, the whole-souled sentiment goes back to ancient, unremembered roots.

Yet Dick Diver's involvement in the war, of which the Second Battle of the Marne was one of the major engagements, had been only peripheral. His medical studies completed, he had been assigned for a year to a neurological unit behind the lines. However, this minimal involvement is historically and symbolically appropriate. This was a European war, which America joined late. It was a war between people with a common cultural heritage and shared memories of similar experiences: British boys who had studied the German philosopher Kant at German universities and venerated Wagner; German youths who had watched French ballet and drunk champagne in Paris on vacation; Austrians who summered on the French Riviera and read Shakespeare. It was a war between people whose religious and cultural affiliations crossed national boundaries and whose commercial rivalries split families.

Dick's understanding of the complex tangle of personal and public values that made this "love battle" came to him second hand, so to speak, partly through his European education as a Rhodes scholar at Oxford and a *Privatdocent* at Zurich. Speaking to his friends at the Marne battle site, he says, "All my beautiful lovely safe world blew itself up here with a great gust of high explosive love." He speaks as an American looking back on a European civilization from which his own cultural values were taken, values lost and destroyed in the great love battle. His illustrations of what constituted that lovely safe world now lost—"postcards of the Crown Prince and his fiancée, and little cafés in Valence and beer gardens in Unter den Linden. . . . country deacons bowling and marraines in Marseilles and girls seduced in the back lanes of Wurtemberg and Westphalia"—nostalgically confirm the European values, a confirmation reinforced by Abe North, the cynical American. Abe burlesques Dick's romantic nostalgia. "The war spirit's getting into me again," he says. "I have a hundred years of Ohio love behind me and I'm going to bomb out this trench."

In a sense—and it is an important sense—*Tender Is the Night* is a book about the ethical significance of cultural differences between Europe and America. For all his Rhodes scholarship and study in Zurich, Dick Diver is an American. He is pictured at the beginning of the book—an image that Fitzgerald returns to at the end, emphasizing and reinforcing it—as General Grant awaiting, in his general store in Galena, his call "to an intricate destiny." The image is a significant one, for General Grant is specifically alluded to at the Marne battle site. And the allusion is antithetical. The kind of battle he is there credited with inventing—"just . . . mass butchery"—was not the "love battle" of the Second Marne. Evidently Grant's call to an "intricate destiny" was, for Fitzgerald, not met. "Intricate" is the key word here. It is the kind of destiny a love battle requires. And the mass butchery of a mere professional soldier does not fit the requirement.

The relationships explored here are subtle and complex. For with the "lovely safe" European world blown up "with a great gust of explosive love" at the Second Battle of the Marne, a tremendous shift of values occurred. Dick Diver, the educated American, inherited the fragmented values of that exploded world. It is not he but his Swiss colleague and counterpart, Dr. Franz Gregorovius, who is the "mere professional." Franz's personal life, with his marriage to a mousey bourgeois *Haus-frau*, is more or less completely disjunct from his professional life. It is he, because he is the late inheritor of a long European family tradition of scientific research, who is the mere minder of the store, or clinic. Dick, on the other hand, is the brilliant researcher whose intricate destiny seems to await him. But in marrying his patient, wedding public and private life, he fails to achieve that destiny. He fails as surely as, in Fitzgerald's conception of him, Grant did. But his failure is of a different kind. Grant's failure is the failure of the mere professional, who could indifferently butcher hordes in the pursuit of a public end. Diver's failure is in the reduction of a public career to the care of a rich sick woman whom he marries and whose life becomes, in effect, his career.

It is interesting to observe, in the light of the foregoing, Nicole's response to Dick's guided tour of the Marne battlefield. (Broken herself, she is, in a sense, his battlefield. Through her life in the clinic, she establishes a relationship with the darker underside of that close, intimate European life that Dick has so happily pictured, her own perverse seduction qualifying the essentially innocent seductions in the "back lanes of Wurtemberg and Westphalia.") And she notes, with implications for her own deteriorating relationship with Dick, his reductive manipulation of that terrible historical event. "He had made," she observes, "a quick study of the whole affair, simplifying it always until it bore a faint resemblance to one of his own parties." On the other hand, Rosemary, the innocent American motion-picture ingenue who is soon to become Dick's mistress, to be a "gust of high explosive love" on Dick's private battlefield, has no insight into either Dick or his lost world. When he questions her about his blown lovely world, she responds, "I don't know. . . . You know everything."

Both responses are curiously ambivalent yet exactly appropriate. Nicole is, in fact, only subliminally critical of Dick, who has made her world for her, when she compares his simplifications of the Battle of the Marne to his party arrangements. Those arrangements are, after all, superb. Constitutive of her world, they are his *raison d'être*. They are the "everything" that he "knows." Providing a private alternative to the lovely, safe pre-1914 world that was destroyed in the war, those arrangements create, for Dick Diver as for Fitzgerald, the illusion of a happily stable world. However limited, moreover, it is the real world of social action, a world in which Fitzgerald sought to excel, seeking recognition as a man of action as well as artist, or man of words.

Nicole's dissatisfaction with Dick increases as she comes to see the control that his knowledge assures slip. And it will slip for a variety of reasons, one of them being that the inhabitants of that circumscribed party world will grow beyond it. They will recognize that the beauty and stability of Dick's world is illusory. It is the product of a confined world based on wealth and power that Dick only *seems* to control. Actually, that power is the Warrens'. And it will revert to them. Nicole will get well. She will seek action in the large world and find in Tommy Barban a lover whose violence abolishes the confines of the small world in which she has lived

And, of course, Dick's knowledge cannot penetrate Rosemary's "innocence." "You know everything," she says, balancing between adulation and indifference like an empty-headed schoolgirl with a crush on her teacher. Not that Rosemary is stupid. She is shrewd in her childishness and acquires worldliness without losing her innocence. When Dick, stung by Collis Clay's stories about Rosemary's "wild" history, confronts her with questions, his intelligence extorts meaningless confessions. Like her mother, the "wise" American who turns her daughter loose for appropriately enlarging experience, Rosemary, whose wisdom is amoral, is not to be measured by the narrow gauge of Dick's moral intelligence. How should it measure her? The moral world is a self-inhibiting one, limited by its own prescriptions. The American in Europe and the Europeanized American are worlds apart.

To be sure, Dick judges Rosemary and finds her lacking. "She's an infant," he tells Nicole. But one can't be sure whether this is a true judgment or an assertion made for Nicole's benefit and to disguise his real relationship with Rosemary. He comes to recognize that "she's not as intelligent as" he had thought. About her he detects "a persistent aroma of the nursery." But his failure to act in accordance with that insight is another indication of his loss of control, a weakening of the moral fiber that ends in the dissolution of his little world. Succumbing to the primitive, amoral nursery world, to the world of impulse, he seduces the "infant," or allows himself to be seduced, reenacting thereby the role of Nicole's father.

We perhaps judge Dick too harshly, make his decline insufficiently clear, by describing his world—the world at Tarmes, where the action of the book centers—as a world of parties. That world is, in fact, a lovely world, the parties being but the heightened essence of a joyous conviviality that transforms ordinary human relations. The effect of that transformation is best seen in the contrast between the McKisco group—newcomers on the beach at Tarmes—and the group surrounding the Divers when Rosemary first comes on the scene and observes both constellations.

The former group, ludicrously out of keeping with their environment, mince about the beach, huddle beneath inadequate parasols, or flounder about in the shallows, "batting" the Mediterranean in a stiff-armed travesty of the crawl. White-fleshed beneath the unfamiliar sun and variously accoutered in everything from full evening regalia to tights too skimpy to cover brash navels, they warn Rosemary, who is also, as a newcomer, pale-fleshed and silly-looking in a peignoir, against the intensity of the sun and the dangers of the water. "I say," exclaims bald, monocled Campion, a man "of indeterminate nationality" speaking English with a slow Oxford drawl, "they have sharks out beyond the raft."

Obtrusively friendly, they appropriate Rosemary for her celebrity value, let her in on an imagined plot supposedly contrived by the Divers to discredit them, and annoy her with their bitterness, boasting, and pusillanimity. When Rosemary sees Abe North swim expertly off from the raft and remarks on his skill, Violet McKisco responds with a violence that surprises Rosemary, "Well, he's a rotten musician." Her husband grudgingly agrees, grudging the agreement not the meanness of the remark.

Violet McKisco uses the gambit as an opportunity to

proclaim her preference for George Antheil—Antheil, the avant-garde composer, and Joyce—the former because she condescendingly assumes that no one from Hollywood will know of him, and the latter because it provides the chance to parade her husband's pitiful accomplishment: he's written "the first criticism of *Ulysses* that ever appeared in America."

Actually, McKisco has another string to his diminutive bow. He's writing a novel. "It's on the idea of *Ulysses*," naturally. "Only," as Violet McKisco observes, "instead of taking twenty-four hours my husband takes a hundred years. He takes a decayed old French aristocrat and puts him in contrast with the mechanical age—" At this point, mercifully, McKisco shuts her up, not wanting "the idea" to be given away prior to publication. The idea, no less!

The dialogue conveys the quality of this group of empty, pretentious arrivistes. Actually, lacking cohesiveness of any sort, it is hardly a group. Rather it is a chaotic agglomeration of disparate types, comprising effeminate young men, one of those elderly " 'good sports' preserved by an imperviousness to experience and a good digestion into another generation," women of disheartening intensity—detritus washed up on the beach of what will soon, unfortunately, be a popular resort.

But it is not yet a popular resort. It is the Divers' creation. And we see them, tan and casual in their beach attire, sunning, swimming, caught up in "the web of some pleasant interrelation" that seems to give purpose and direction "even in their absolute immobility." There is an implicit fullness in their lives, so that to Rosemary, "It seemed that there was no life anywhere in all this expanse of coast except under the filtered sunlight of those umbrellas, where something went on amid the color and the murmur."

"Some pleasant interrelation," "something went on" —the phrases suggest a mystery. But there is no mystery other than the sense of completeness that is conferred upon even the most trivial of pleasures by the harmonious and dignified ordering of civilized life. The mystery is implicit in what the Divers have created—a society. And of course the breath and finer spirit of that society is a party. To Rosemary, fresh from America, a Diver party is a kind of ultimate "homecoming . . . a return from the derisive and salacious improvisations of the frontier" to the refreshment of the paradisical garden at Tarmes. Thus Fitzgerald contrasts American and European values and indicates the relationship between them.

The Divers subtly emerge from behind the motley screen of the McKiscos through Rosemary's bright but naïve consciousness. Now she describes the party, a party in which the crude idiosyncrasies of the participants are blended and transformed under the sure guidance of the Divers. Dick especially takes up the slack of ordinary social relations, pulling those relations taut into ideal alignment. Fitzgerald described Gatsby as springing from "his Platonic conception of himself." Dick Diver's party might be thought of as the social extension of that idea, the idea that an ultimate reality exists in an ideal conceptual world, quite apart from its actualization in the ever-changing world about us. Plato's *Symposium*, celebrating human discourse at the highest level of perfection—a kind of ideal banquet or party—gives it birth. Within its magical ambience, the guests—even the dreadful McKiscos and their friends— are "daringly lifted above conviviality into the rarer atmosphere. . . ." As Rosemary pictures the scene, "The table seemed to have risen a little toward the sky like a mechanical dancing platform, giving the people around it a sense of being alone with each other in the dark universe, nourished by its only food, warmed by its only lights."

The trick—"a trick of the heart" Dick is later to call it—is accomplished as if on signal, as Diver "began suddenly to warm and glow and expand. . . ." Earlier in the evening he had overlooked a breach of manners, leaving it to solve itself. "He was saving his newness for a larger effort," we are told, "waiting a more significant moment for his guests to be conscious of a good time." The moment arrives, and he "opened the gate to his amusing world," winning "everyone quickly with an exquisite consideration and a politeness that moved so fast and intuitively that it could be examined only in its effect." Rosemary notes that "detachment from the world" has been attained. It is a remarkable experience, convincing people that Diver "made special reservations about them, recognizing the proud uniqueness of their destinies. . . ." He seems, says Rosemary, to want to make up to them "for anything they might still miss from that country well left behind." The country "well left behind" is, of course, the actual world of postwar Europe, the broken fragments of Diver's lovely safe world blown up in the war. The fact that it is broken, fragmented, blown up, is a function of its tight restrictiveness. It was "safe" only for the exploitative Warrens—self-centered Baby and her corrupt, hypocritical father. Hence the need to rescue the fragments—the victims like Nicole —and to reconstruct a world patterned on its stability but lacking its dangerous oppressiveness. This was a job equally incumbent on Diver and on Fitzgerald. For the latter it was important both as an artist, whose function is to create order from chaos, and as a man who had always felt himself to be relegated to the fringes of a privileged society of wealth, power, and beauty.

So the world is well lost. But is it? Wasn't it well lost —for love? But that is what Dick has. That is the motivating magic at the center of his social world. Unless it, too, is just "a trick of the heart." "My politeness is a trick of the heart," he confesses to Rosemary's mother, who admires his good manners. And he asserts, "There's too much good manners." Has his love been mere politeness, good manners, concern for Nicole's disordered feelings? Is this what he has spent his life for? "If you spend your life sparing people's feelings and feeding their vanity," Dick observes, "you get so you can't distinguish what *should* be respected in them."

Or in yourself, he might have added. For the level of his excitement about people, the extraordinary virtuosity of his relationship with them, reaches as his wife notes, "an intensity out of proportion to their importance." Dick expends emotions with the lavishness with which his wife spends money, the indiscriminate extravagance of the very rich. "The very rich are different from you and me," Fitzgerald observed elsewhere. Surely Dick Diver's emotional spendthriftism indicates that Hemingway missed the point of the observation in responding, "Yes, they have more money." Money frees Dick from the demands of the external world, allowing him to make a world after the pattern of his heart, a world dictated by the heart's extravagance rather than the exigencies and pressures of society.

But what of the pressures of the heart itself and of the heart's tricks? What of the reaction to "the waste and extravagance involved"? Looking at her husband in one of his characteristic moods, Nicole says, "He sometimes looked back with awe at the carnivals of affection he had given, as a general might gaze upon a massacre he had ordered to satisfy an impersonal blood lust." The wheel comes full circle. We are back with General Grant and his mass butchery, excluded from the intricate destiny of the love battle by his mere professionalism. A soldier, his business was war. Dr. Dick Diver's whole business, to which he brings, paradoxically, the impersonal lust of the professional, has become love.

Whether or not Dick Diver has been corrupted by wealth is perhaps an open question, though there is no doubt in Baby Warren's mind that he has been bought when she tells her sister Nicole at the end of the novel, dismissing any emotional claims that Dick may have on her, "That's what he was educated for." Actually, the question of what he was educated for is much to the point. Was it for service? If so, of what kind? The service of love? Should the emphasis then lie on service or love, on professionalism or the good life, on public duty or private fulfillment? To put it another way, the book turns upon the question of the meaning of integrity and the problem of innocence in a world that, following the debacle of World War I, has lost the ability to articulate public codes in meaningful private terms.

After all, the central fact of the book is the rape of Nicole as a child by her father, a substantial, respectable figure of the great world who tells his other daughter that he "would have shot" the boy who, he allows her to think, is responsible for Nicole's condition. But himself the culprit, he tries to sneak away from Dohmler's sanitarium without providing the key to Nicole's illness. "Peasant," Dohmler says to himself when he hears the story, placing old man Warren's "innocence."

Nicole's cure is effected by transference of her love for her father, shattered by his violation of her, to Dr. Diver, the innocent father figure whose cure restores her, ultimately and paradoxically, to the very antithesis of Diver's world, the world of violence Tommy Barban represents.

Dick Diver's reenactment of the crime of Nicole's father with the "infant" Rosemary has already been mentioned. But there are further incongruities in that relationship. Rosemary is, to begin with, an "innocent" movie star. When her part in the story begins, she has just scored a big success as the ingenue in a film called "Daddy's Girl." Carefully brought up by her acute and sensitive mother, she is encouraged in her amorous design upon Dick by her mother, who in her innocent worldliness thinks only of the good such an affair can do her daughter. Moreover, Rosemary is rumored to have had a shady past by the naive college boy Collis Clay, whom she keeps on the hook. In any case, her appeal to Dick for love is both shockingly direct and astonishingly gauche. "Take me," she whispers when she finally gets him alone in her hotel room. And when he fails to respond,

> "Go on," she whispered. "Oh, please go on, whatever they do. I don't care if I don't like it— I never expected to—I've always hated to think about it but now I don't. I want you to."

This appeal takes place in a section of the book called "Casualties." Dick resists. The casualty, he feels, would be not Rosemary but Nicole, whom he loves and would betray by such a casual affair. So he merely kisses Rosemary, saying, "Nicole mustn't suffer—she loves me and I love her. . . . And I mean love . . . . Active love." Actually the casualty is that love—though we are not to realize it until later in the book when the affair with Rosemary is consummated—

and hence himself, for he is intensely committed to his love for Nicole. "Nicole and I have got to go on together," he says. "In a way that's more important than just wanting to go on." But he becomes a casualty. He falls in love with Rosemary, a love that is not consummated until several years later, when Rosemary is another woman fully experienced now and accepting Dick merely as a casual lover.

Rosemary is not the sole measure of Dick Diver's corruption, though she is a central measure of it, since his affair with her represents a deviation from that service of the heart that is, for good and ill, at the very core of his being—"in a way that's more important than just wanting to go on." In fact, in the version of *Tender Is the Night* published by Fitzgerald in the spring of 1934, and still the better version of the book,[1] we see the Divers first through Rosemary's young eyes. The effect is a subtle and complex one, magnifying Dick and idealizing his marriage with Nicole, yet hinting at vague corruptions in the relationship, seemingly attributable to Nicole and colored by our uncertainty respecting Rosemary. As Nicole's past and Rosemary's future are revealed to us in a context of violence, debauchery, and death, we realize how tenuous was the paradisical idyll created by Dick in a chaotic universe, even as his own fallibility becomes more and more manifest.

Significantly the reader's first view of Dick is as a kind of serene park attendant in paradise, with rake and shovel, cultivating his sandy garden. In the last scene he

---

[1] Annoyed by the commercial failure of *Tender Is the Night*, Fitzgerald revised it following publication, substituting a strictly chronological ordering of events for the psychologically more apt version originally published, beginning with Rosemary's observation of the Divers at Tarmes. The revised version was published posthumously. Its sole advantage over the version originally published is clarity of plot.

exits as a shaky dethroned pope, blessing with a theatrical gesture the peopled desert of a flourishing resort. In that juxtaposition lies the history of Dick Diver's decline: an increase in tippling, a disinclination for work, physical deterioration, failure of discrimination, loss of friends, bankruptcy of emotion.

For many readers, everything in the novel springs from or reflects this progressive bankruptcy. And there is much to be said for this view. Thus Abe North in his own decline anticipates Dick's when he announces: "Tired of friends. The thing to have is sycophants." With Dick we move through dooms of love, from love that is a giving of the self—for Nicole; to love that is a self-indulgence—for Rosemary; to love that is a contrivance necessary for self-preservation—as he strives half-heartedly to win Mary North by "working over" her at the very end of the book. But Dick tires of the effort, and cynical laughter wells up within him. Not for him the desperate pragmatic wisdom of Robert Frost's provision against loneliness:

> Better to go down dignified
> With boughten friendship at your side
> Than none at all. Provide, provide!

Like Abe North, Dick comes to equate friend and sycophant. But he'll buy no more friends with his effort, nor permit himself to be bought.

Actually Dick had worked over all his women, especially Nicole. He had come to see the result of that work, rising from the emotional wreckage of her early life, as a fine tower. But during one of Nicole's lapses into madness, he laments:

> It was awful that such a fine tower should not be

erected, only suspended, suspended from him. . . .
she was Dick too, the drought in the marrow of
his bones. He could not watch her disintegrations
without participating in them.

Recalling Zelda's rivalry with Fitzgerald and her accusations against him, one cannot help but see in this episode, drawing upon the most agonizing events in the lives of the Fitzgeralds, the intimate bonding of repressed and transferred emotions, projected penis envy and fears of sexual inadequacy being mingled in a mixed metaphor of bones and buildings with hopes and fears of wholeness for both partner and self. The obvious sexual implications of the situation are alluded to by Dick, who asserts that between his discovery of Nicole, "flowering under a stone on the Zürichsee," and his meeting with Rosemary, "the spear had been blunted." It appears that the intimate love battle can be fought too close, binding opponents together as one, destroying identity, and draining vitality without providing an opportunity for the requisite thrust and counterthrust of normal healthy heterosexual relations. (One mordantly comic illustration of the need for freedom from such destructive possessiveness comes early in the novel when a distraught girl shoots her lover—through his identification card!)

Suspended towers and blunted spears appropriately image for Dick, the cultivated, highly civilized expatriate, his deteriorating situation. But more vulgar and vital images signalize the end of his affair in a hilarious vignette toward the close of the book. The episode occurs as Nicole and Tommy Barban prepare to leave the waterfront hotel in which they have spent the night together, marking Nicole's break with Dick. Regaining healthy independence, Nicole pits her unscrupulousness against Dick's moralities. She has welcomed the anarchy of her barbarous lover, rejecting the civilized velleities of Dick. Now the *Cr-ack—Boom-mm* of the big gun on an American battleship splits the air with its imperative of duty, recalling its sailors. As they leave, two girls rush into Tommy and Nicole's room and out onto the balcony. One of them hoists her skirt and rips off her step-ins, tearing them into a pink flag to wave at her departing lover. "As Tommy and Nicole left the room," we are told, "it still fluttered against the blue sky." And Francis Scott Key Fitzgerald questions, "Oh, say can you see the tender color of remembered flesh—while at the stern of the battleship arose in rivalry the Star-Spangled Banner."

The tender color of remembered flesh versus the stern call of duty. How absolute a juxtaposition. And how comic a reduction. A reduction that only *opera buffa*—and life —demand. So Dick Diver, unequal to the demand, retreats to the American wilderness to await, once more like Grant, the call to his intricate destiny. But Grant, we remember, had failed according to Fitzgerald's conception of the nature of that destiny, having made too simple a response to its intricate demands. What then remains? For Dick has failed for reasons opposite from Grant's—or almost so. He has not failed—as Grant did—to meet the call of his destiny with a response sufficiently intricate to match that call. On the contrary, his response has been too intricate, subtle, and complex. He has been defeated by the raw crudity of life itself, by Nicole's return to health and her appetite for direct experience—the passion and violence of Tommy Barban. And of course by his own inability to sustain the level of response his destiny called forth. He responds appropriately but insufficiently.

One recalls the woman whom Dick treated at the sanitarium on the Zugersee, nursing her through her final illness. An American painter, seeking to explore "the frontiers of consciousness," plagued by questions of sexual identity, and suffering from maddening eczema, her problems and her anguish are closely related to Zelda and Scott Fitzgerald's and to Nicole and Dick Diver's. And her destiny is—death, into which she takes the intricate question which she sees her suffering as somehow symbolic of. In the majesty of her suffering and in the compassion of Dick's response is the only affirmation. Except perhaps for the exploration of the frontiers of consciousness that is the artist's justification and that was "too tough a game" for her. As it was for F. Scott Fitzgerald.

6

Obstinately Unhorrified

"—And then, ten years this side of forty-nine, I suddenly realized that I had prematurely cracked."

Fitzgerald gives the time and occasion in "The Crack-Up," a confessional piece published in February 1936 in *Esquire* magazine. He had just recovered from an attack of tuberculosis that was serious enough to require the services of a top specialist and a spring and summer of complete rest in Asheville, North Carolina. Then "suddenly, surprisingly," he got better, "—And cracked like an old plate as soon as I heard the news." The description is dramatic and convincing, but Dick Diver's analysis of himself is probably closer to what happened to Fitzgerald than the author's confessional piece. Describing his own deterioration to Rosemary, Dick says, "The change came a long way back—but at first it didn't show. The manner remains intact for some time after the morale cracks." Fitzgerald admits as much later in "The Crack-Up" when he says "that every act of life from the morning tooth-brush to the friend at dinner had become an effort. I saw that for a long time I had not liked people and things, but only followed the rickety old pretense of liking. I saw that even my love for those closest to me was become only an attempt to love, that my casual relations—with an editor, a tobacco seller, the child of a friend, were only what I remembered I *should* do, from other days."

Fitzgerald dates the change in himself to 1934, but surely it goes back long before that. Zelda's brief, abortive love affair with Edouard Jozan had occurred ten years earlier, and things hadn't been the same between Zelda and Fitzgerald since. They had quarrelled stormily over the intervening years, and though they had made up over and over again, bitter residues of pain and anguish accumulated in both of them. Moreover, Zelda's breakdown had occasioned profound feelings of guilt in Fitzgerald as he examined his relationship with his wife and assessed his responsibility for her condition.

In addition, Fitzgerald felt his command of his craft slipping. He had worked for almost a decade on a single novel, altering, abandoning, resuming, reconceiving, struggling with the demons of despair as he tried to finish it.

And there was his alcoholism. Like most alcoholics, he tried to conceal his addiction. In "The Crack-Up" he claimed that he had "not tasted so much as a glass of beer for six months." The facts were otherwise. Indeed, in moments of candor he confessed as much. In one such moment he lamented to Maxwell Perkins, "I would give anything if I hadn't had to write Part III of *Tender Is the Night* entirely on stimulant." In fact, since his return from Europe in 1931, his physical condition had deteriorated to such a degree that he collapsed on several occasions and was in and out of the hospital for varying periods, with what appeared to be the onset of cirrhosis of the liver. He even had an arrangement with a doctor friend, a kind of alcoholic early-warning system, requiring him to call the doctor when he began to drink, so that he could be placed under surveillance, given appropriate drugs, or hospitalized as his condition necessitated.

To be sure, it was in 1934, or thereabouts, that his situation became critical. For one thing, his third novel had finally been published. Its completion had been a test of his failing powers. And he had won through, with great effort and at much cost. But *Tender Is the Night* got bad reviews. And it sold only about 13,000 copies. Moreover, the Depression was on, and Fitzgerald could no longer command high prices for the popular stories that he used to turn out to keep himself solvent. Debts began to accumulate, eventually reaching the sum of forty thousand dollars.

But the hardest blow of all came in January 1934, when Zelda had her third breakdown. There was a suicide attempt, institutionalization, catatonia. Partial recovery was effected, only to be followed by relapses. For the next six years, Zelda was to spend most of her time in hospitals and sanitariums. "I left my capacity for hope," Fitzgerald was later to say, "on the little roads that led to Zelda's sanitarium."

Not hope alone, the very capacity for hope seemed lost. This was surely that "dark night of the soul" that Fitzgerald described in "Handle with Care," the second of the three pieces published in *Esquire*, recounting what he called "the disintegration" of his "own personality." In such a dark night there seems to be no morning. Life has no purpose. All values are lost. It is, he wails, "always three o'clock in the morning" and "a forgotten package has the same tragic importance as a death sentence." He had "a feeling," he says elsewhere in the piece, "that I was standing at twilight on a deserted range, with an empty rifle in my hands and the targets down. No problem set—simply a silence with only the sound of my own breathing."

Loneliness and despair are magnified by recollection of the intensity of feeling that bound him and Zelda together. Even after years of conflict and of separation resulting from Zelda's madness, the feeling persisted—in both of them. Zelda expresses it with heart-breaking poignancy in a letter written during a lucid interval several years after her third breakdown. "Dearest and always Dearest Scott," she begins her letter to him. And after touching on her own shattered emptiness, on the joys and dreams of the past, and on an impossible vision of a tranquil and productive future, she concludes, using the nickname by which she sometimes called him:

> I want you to be happy—if there were any justice you would be happy—maybe you will be anyway.
> Oh, Do-Do, Do Do—
> I love you anyway—even if there isn't any me or any love or even any life—
> I love you.

But there was to be no happiness. And as Zelda sank further into madness, there was in fact very little of her left. As for Fitzgerald himself, he says in "Handle with Care," "A man does not recover from such jolts—he becomes a different person and, eventually, the new person finds new things to care about."

Eventually he did. There was his daughter, Scottie, whose education he had to provide for. In 1937 he went to

Hollywood again, this time to stay. As a screen writer he did not have much success, but he made a living and he got to know the industry well. He also got to know Sheilah Graham, a columnist with a checkered background, an engaging naïveté, and a strong will, and established a liaison with her. Finally there was his writing.

In a letter written just after the publication of *Tender Is the Night,* which he did not like—he was to come to like it later—because he thought it cheaply confessional and dangerously self-indulgent, Hemingway urged: "Forget your personal tragedy. . . . when you get the damned hurt use it—don't cheat with it. . . . All we are is writers and what we should do is write." Fitzgerald had been deeply wounded by the letter, for he knew the true value of the book. (He was always to consider it his best.) He also knew that he hadn't cheated. *Tender Is the Night* is not a self-indulgent confession but an exploration, based on intimate experience, of the corruption of the heart. Hemingway had missed the point. But Fitzgerald had always respected his judgment. And now at the end of his career he assumed the burden of that judgment. In "Pasting It Together," the third of the series of articles he wrote for *Esquire* about the disintegration of his personality, he concluded with an observation about the new person he thought he had become: "I have now at last become a writer only."

His conclusion is erroneous. But it points to a new quality that his writing will take on in his last years. "I am not a great man," he wrote his daughter in 1939, "but sometimes I think the impersonal and objective quality of my talent . . . has some sort of epic grandeur." *The Last Tycoon,* though it grew out of personal experience, has that "impersonal and objective quality" in a way that no other book of Fitzgerald's except *The Great Gatsby* does.

There are other resemblances between the two books, extending even to the titles, both of which celebrate individualism in hyperbolic terms bordering on the grotesque yet touched with pathos In fact, *The Last Tycoon* is, in a sense, *The Great Gatsby* turned inside out, with the career of the man of action no longer merely hinted at but brought to the focus of attention and examined in detail. Jay Gatsby's ambiguous profession is a mystery based on an American illusion and fed by his love for Daisy, which destroys him. Monroe Stahr's love is a ghostly memory, flaring into new life with Kathleen Moore in the midst of a destructive career as a creator of American illusion.

There are, however, great differences between the two books. For one thing, *Gatsby*, a relatively short and tightly structured book, is a magnificently finished novel, every detail carefully articulated and fully resonant. *The Last Tycoon* is incomplete, unfinished through the circumstance of Fitzgerald's untimely death. Fewer than six chapters of the projected work exist, telling less than half the story Fitzgerald outlined. Moreover, though the extant chapters had been much rewritten, almost every episode contains marginal comments in Fitzgerald's handwriting, suggesting further revision or indicating discontent with the state of the episode in question. In fact, at the head of the last draft of Chapter One the author wrote: "Rewrite from mood. Has become stilted with rewriting. Don't look. Rewrite from mood."

Thus it appears that many of the infelicities in the book might have been eliminated in further revisions. It may be captious to criticize what might have been changed. But one can't say, "Don't look." All one has is what Fitzgerald left. There will never be more. And it seems unlikely that certain aspects of the book would have been changed. The point of view, for example, has been established. One sees the events in the story of Monroe Stahr, a great motion-picture producer, through the love-stricken eyes of Cecilia Brady, college-age daughter of his partner and enemy. It is she who tells with adolescent anguish of Stahr's double devotion: to work and to the memory of his dead wife Minna. One sees through her adoring eyes the harmony that Stahr creates out of the chaos of elements that comprises the movie industry, and we learn of his problems with actors, cameramen, writers, moguls of the industry, technicians, union organizers, and others. Even Stahr's love affair with Kathleen Moore, a woman encountered by chance during a flood on the studio lot, where he notices her resemblance to his dead wife, comes to us through Cecilia Brady. She, too, reports what would seem to be the end of the affair, with Kathleen's marriage, and forewarns us of Stahr's imminent demise.

Cecilia, who thus unfolds the story, "has been brought up in pictures," but is not a part of them. "My father was in the picture business," she says—placing him as the antithesis of Stahr, who is the artistic conscience and soul of the industry—"as another man might be in cotton or steel, and I took it tranquilly." She is being educated in the East—at Bennington College, in fact. So she can say of gaudy commercial Hollywood, cesspool of lost integrities and center of artistic philistinism, "I knew what you were supposed to think of it but I was obstinately unhorrified."

Combining passionate insight and objective knowledge, Cecilia is an ideal observer of Stahr's career of genius, that of a true star in a specious firmament. However, Stahr's private life, his love affair with Kathleen Moore, has to be imagined, projected from hints supplied by others and eked out by intuition. Actually that affair, which is more explicitly sexual than anything else in Fitzgerald, is not badly handled, the rapidity and intensity of Stahr's involvement being saved from sentimentality by reflection through Cecilia's consciousness. Fitzgerald even manages to bridge the gap between Stahr the wary and disenchanted man of experience and Stahr the passionate lover. As a matter of fact, that disjunction is close to the center of interest in the book, which is concerned with a man, like Fitzgerald himself, who had loved and lost and who, without ever recovering from the jolt, becomes a different person and "finds new things to care about." Since Kathleen resembles Minna, Stahr's dead wife, the new is not completely new. And obviously the different person who finds Kathleen on a studio lot is still very much the same man as the one who loved Minna. Altering a pronoun, one might say of Stahr what Faulkner says of Dilsey in *The Sound and the Fury*: he endured. In a world of annihilating change, that is no small feat, as both authors knew.

And Stahr doesn't merely endure; he prevails, dominating and molding an industry, giving it what solid values it has, in spite of the venality, incompetence, stupidity, and greed of the parasitic exploiters who infest it. His career, based on that of Irving Thalberg, the great Hollywood motion-picture producer in the twenties and thirties, is an exemplary one. More than a model of a modern major producer, he is a heroic individualist in a shoddy world, holding that world together, shaping it for itself and giving to its tinsel show a real grandeur by the power of his will. That he does so at the cost of himself, driving his sick body by controlled effort, gives pathos to his portrait. And his continued love of life, his daily defiance of death, and his victory over the ghosts of the past, as evinced in his love for Kathleen, deepens the pathos to tragedy.

Given such high aims so nearly realized, Fitzgerald can be forgiven much, particularly since the flaws in his work might well have been eliminated had he had time to give the kind of attention to details that he had devoted to the central substance of his book. And there are flaws. There is, for example, a certain awkwardness in his manipulation of point of view. One is too much aware of the author shifting gears as Cecilia slips back from a speculative presentation of Stahr's love affair to engage the solid stuff of his Hollywood career. She is made to say things like: "This is Cecilia taking up the story." And "This is Cecilia taking up the narrative in person," creaking transitions that Thackeray would not have used in the adolescence of the novel. On one occasion, she confesses, "I knew nothing about any of this," referring to an episode that had just been recounted. And she is used, more by Fitzgerald than by Stahr, improbably, to set up a meeting with an important Communist party member, principally so that she can be on the scene to report it. The devices in question are awkward and mechanical, calling attention to the methods of literary fabrication rather than permitting us to get through those methods the sense of life they should convey.

There are other flaws as well. There is, for instance, an encounter early in the novel between Stahr and George Boxley, an English novelist who has been hired to write for the movies. Boxley has not been doing well, his scenarios consisting of dialogue with no action, no pictures for the camera to record. In a brief interview, Stahr gives him, off the top of his head, a pictorial scene that might be effective instruction in a freshman writing class but that any novelist would have learned as a lesson long before the publication of his first book. The scene is all wrong. Not only is the lesson too simple; it is too naively accepted by the sophisticated, literary Englishman, who approached the interview with extreme hostility. In something under two pages, he is eating out of Stahr's hand—eating pap.

Moreover, one of the lessons that Stahr provides Boxley with is the lesson that cheap or extravagant sensationalism—duelling or falling down wells—is not necessary for effective pictorial presentation. But when the interview occurs, we have just been through an earthquake and a studio flood in which a woman floats into Stahr's life, sitting on the head of a drifting statue. Shortly, a cameraman is to attempt suicide and break his arm jumping from Stahr's balcony. Cecilia is to discover something of her father's nature when his secretary tumbles unconscious—and stark naked—from a closet in which she has been concealed. An important turn in the plot is to depend on a letter accidentally misplaced and later discovered. Kathleen gets married between chapters and informs her lover of the night before by telegram the next morning. And an orang-outang posing as President McKinley calls Stahr on the telephone at his unfinished beach house!

To be sure, not all of this is ineffective. In fact, the quantity of bizarre action in the novel helps to define the crazy world of Hollywood. But it certainly provides an awkward context for Stahr's lesson to Boxley. And it poses questions perhaps better not raised if we are to accept Stahr at the author's evaluation as a moviemaker of genius, questions about the adequacy of his genius to interpret his milieu. For he seems to be unaware of the bizarreness of the world about him.

Actually, however, the movies of the twenties and thirties didn't interpret the complex and often bizarre land from which they sprang in any direct and representational way. They provided simplifying fables, popular myths that people took to their hearts as guides in the midst of their confusion. That is what Stahr provided. Thus in a depression economy, with hundreds of thousands unemployed and great bitterness manifest between employee and employer, Stahr insists on having the feminine lead, in a new picture he is making about a stenographer, full of dumb admiration for her boss. She stands for "health, vitality, ambition, and love," and Stahr will have no trace of revolutionary discontent in her makeup. The boss in the movie, in turn, despite Stahr's own concern with serious labor trouble in the studios, is not to be "jittery," as bosses of the period often were, with good reason. In fact, there is to be no doubt or hesitation in any character, although this was a period in American history filled with uncertainty. This is a happy story, Stahr affirms, criticizing his underlings who have been attempting to infuse "reality" into his picture. "When I want to do a Eugene O'Neill play," he continues, "I'll buy one."

Stahr sounds like a stereotyped movie mogul, a stupid, insensitive man obsessed with money and power. But he is more complex than that. His limitations are apparent enough. For example, in preparing for the meeting with the Communist party member, he accepts a suggestion that the script department of the studio get up "a two-page treatment of the *Communist Manifesto*"! That's something like putting *War and Peace* or *Moby-Dick* onto a five-minute film strip, or making Lincoln's Gettysburg Address into a musical comedy. Happily he doesn't read it, being, we are told, "a rationalist who did his own reasoning without benefit of books." In fact, Stahr's only reading is movie scenarios. He knows neither history, philosophy, art, nor literature. "Who are they?" he asks Pete Zavras, his Greek cameraman, when Zavras, in gratitude to Stahr for having saved his career, compares Stahr to Aeschylus and Euripides, Aristophanes, and Menander. They're Greek to Stahr, who thinks maybe they were in the movies. When Kathleen sees herself as a Botticelli, reclining in Stahr's half-finished beach house after making love, he is obviously nonplussed. And when she tells him of her education by an earlier lover, as a preparation for reading Spengler, he questions, "Who was Spengler?"

In point of fact, however, Stahr values education, having had himself no "more than a night-school course in stenography." Zavras's allusions induce him to say, "You make me sorry I didn't get an education." And when Kathleen tells him that she is forgetting everything she had learned, he is shocked, having, we are told, "an intense respect for learning, a racial memory of the old *schules*. . . . 'You shouldn't forget,' " he tells Kathleen. And when she replies, "It was just in place of babies," this conversation follows:

> "You could teach your babies," he said.
> "Could I?"
> "Sure you could. You could give it to them while they were young. When I want to know anything, I've got to ask some drunken writer. Don't throw it away."

Spengler is a modern German philosopher who predicted the disintegration of Western cultural values, particularly those that place a premium on individual accomplishment. Mention of his name serves as an appropriately ironic commentary, in the context of misprized learning and dependence on drunken writers, on Stahr's heroic if unlearned individualism, an individualism soon to be beleaguered by nonentities.

But the fact of the matter is that Spengler has been too

highly valued by Kathleen's erratic, decadent former lover. The pessimistic philosopher of *The Decline of the West* is no guide for a man like Stahr, who has risen from poverty to a position of wealth and power and established an industry in which he struggles to assert the values of health, vitality, ambition, and love. Well might such a man ask, "Who is Spengler?"

Indeed his question is given peculiar force by virtue of a scene in the book following the lovemaking of Stahr and Kathleen. The scene, a kind of coda to their love affair, is dominated by a rich image of plenitude as they walk upon the beach in a tide of swarming grunion with a black man who gathers pails full of the little silvery fish. The black man, who reads Emerson and detests movies, is a minor figure but an important one, for Stahr determines, after the episode, to throw out three or four borderline pictures that were to go into production that week. He sees them now as trash and determines to substitute for them a difficult but worthwhile picture that he had decided to sacrifice. Reasserting his integrity, he says of the picture that he "rescued it for the negro man." It is a rescue that Spengler, with his concept of culture and his belief that "the earth will inevitably fall victim to the colored men," would have found incomprehensible.

Nor is the episode in question the sole index of Stahr's integrity. He has earlier—in Chapter Three of the unfinished novel—demonstrated his superiority to the gross demands of the profit motive at a luncheon conference on a film in production. The film has had problems; production costs have risen, and it is questionable that it will make a large enough profit to justify the increase. Under the circumstances, the senior executives assume that the picture will be dropped. Stahr demurs. The picture will not make its costs, he asserts; it will actually lose money. But it is a quality picture, and Stahr, to the consternation of the senior executives, insists that it be completed.

But a question arises, What is a "worthwhile" or "quality" picture? And—a flaw in the novel—one gets no direct or detailed answer. To be sure, the kind of girl Stahr wants in one of the pictures he is making stands for "health, vitality, ambition and love," as we have seen. These are positive enough values, values embodied in Stahr himself until he lost the first and last elements of the quartet, elements he may recoup with Kathleen. But these elements represent pretty general qualities, and one has no chance to see them adduced in any of Stahr's pictures. As a matter of fact, the glimpses that one gets of Stahr's work reveal him as a skillful craftsman, knowledgeable about technique: suggesting a shot of a boy on a roof to a cameraman; criticizing a close-up of a scene where a star's face has been missed while the camera focused on the top of her head; editing scripts mentally, without using a pencil; taking a director off a job when he's lost control of the picture; putting writers on a script in relays to get desired results without wasting time.

This latter technique, inspired by practical, pecuniary considerations, is in fact the invention of Stahr, who sees himself as a merchant. "I'm a merchant," he says to Wylie White, the writer. "I want to buy what's in your mind." Wylie, quoting Charles Francis Adams, who, like his brother Henry, looked rather sniffishly down his nose at the captains of industry who helped to shape modern America, deplores Stahr's self-description. "You're no merchant," he says. But Stahr persists, placing Adams accurately despite his own lack of history. "Adams was probably a sourbelly," said Stahr. "He wanted to be head man himself, but he didn't have the judgment or else the character." When Wylie replies tartly, "He had brains," Stahr responds, "It takes more than brains."

Indeed it does. For Stahr is a practical man, a man of action who knows what it takes to get things done. That is the point of the little story he tells the pilot in the first chapter on his flight back to the West Coast. Looking down at the mountains, he asks the pilot to suppose himself a railroad builder who has to get a train through the mountains. There are several gaps, one no better than another. "You've got to decide—on what basis? You can't test the best way—except by doing it. So you just do it."

The pilot misses the point, as well he might. After all, he is a pilot, who sees mountains from a different perspective from railroad men. But then, most of the people who surround Stahr miss the point. Wylie White the writer, who is on the flight and who takes Cecilia Brady out to see the Hermitage, Andrew Jackson's old home, when the plane is grounded in Nashville, misses the point. At the very shrine of the "inventor of the Spoils System," which rewarded political support by political office, Wylie seeks preferment through favoritism, trying to gain advancement by making up to Brady's daughter instead of on the basis of his skill as a writer. Moreover, he sees Manny Schwartz, a fallen movie magnate who has accompanied Cecilia and himself to the Hermitage, recouping his power simply because he once belonged to the film-industry oligarchy. Explaining Manny to Cecilia, Wylie says: "Now he's down and out. But he'll be back. You can't flunk out of pictures unless you're a dope or a drunk." But he's wrong. Stahr has already eliminated Schwartz as an incompetent hanger-on. He tells the former producer, "Whatever you're after, the answer is No!" And Manny, with no place in an economy based on productivity, stays behind at the Hermitage and blows his brains out.

The suicide of Manny Schwartz, who "had come a long way from some ghetto to present himself at that raw shrine" of Andrew Jackson, anticipates Stahr's end. For just as Manny, an Old World sycophant, has no place in the world of Jacksonian democracy—"Manny Schwartz and Andrew Jackson—it was hard to say them in the same sentence"—so Stahr, made in the mold of the railroad builders of an earlier day, is something of an anachronism in the era of the airplane. His craftsmanship and his paternalism are alike unmeaning in an industry controlled, increasingly, by big unions on the one hand and on the other by finance capitalists with no interest in or knowledge of the film industry itself.

Stahr is in fact "out of key with his time." An individualist and a man of action, he is the type of the nineteenth-century merchant prince or industrial baron, whose power was based on the fact that he linked the continent with a net of rails, dressed it in cotton, or put it on wheels. Indeed, the people who have been at the studio a long time think of him as "the last of the princes." And Stahr looks upon himself as a Roman. Explaining his conception of ownership and of utility to Brimmer, the Communist, Stahr says: "I never thought that I had more brains than a writer has. But I always thought that his brains *belonged* to me—because I knew how to use them. Like the Romans—I've heard that they never invented things but they knew what to do with them. Do you see? I don't say it's right. But it's the way I've always felt—since I was a boy."

An expert technician, refusing to make moral judgments or to examine too closely the nature of his feelings while attempting to maintain his leadership in a rapidly changing world, Monroe Stahr is in many ways very like Fitzgerald at this stage of his career, who said of himself, "I have now become a writer only" and who deliberately abandoned the close self-analysis that had preoccupied him through much of his work on *Tender Is the Night* for the more objective presentation of *The Last Tycoon*. Fitzgerald might even be seen, in his Hollywood years, as picking the brain of the writer that "belonged" to him in order to adapt what he found to the making of motion pictures. That would account for the image he uses to describe Boxley's reaction to writing for the films—an image of a huge quarry "where even the newly cut marble bore the traces of old pediments, half-obliterated inscriptions of the past."

To be sure, the image applies to the novel, too, especially *The Last Tycoon*, where Gatsby looms behind Stahr, Fitzgerald behind both, and Zelda haunts the pages as the half-obliterated ghost of Stahr's dead wife, who is mirrored in Kathleen Moore, a character based on Fitzgerald's mistress Sheilah Graham.

Lamenting the mass-production techniques of the movies that put a premium on time and don't allow you to "let yourself go," Boxley says, "I keep wishing you could start all over." That was Fitzgerald's wish too, as it is the wish of so many of us. But conditions dictate otherwise. As Stahr says, "There's always some lousy condition." In the movies it's the need to "take people's own favorite folklore and dress it up and give it back to them. . . . Anything beyond that is sugar," as Stahr crudely expresses it.

And in the novel? Much the same. The need to give

back to people the story of a boy's rise from rags to riches, dressed up as Gatsby or Monroe Stahr, and of the love he wins and loses, and of the desire to start all over. But there's always some lousy condition. The girl marries someone else. The gun has a bullet. The plane falls. The heart gives out. Just as in real life. "Look!" Fitzgerald wrote in a letter to his daughter in October 1939. "I have begun to write something that is maybe great, and I'm going to be absorbed in it four or six months. . . . And I think when you read this book, which will encompass the time when you knew me as an adult, you will understand how intensively I knew your world. . . ." Fitzgerald's description is accurate, his evaluation just. But the book was to take more than six months. And he didn't have them.

What remains is five chapters and a bit, plus some notes, sketches, and an outline. But the fragment contains perhaps the best picture of Hollywood ever done. It comes in bits and pieces, like a montage of chaos. Drive-in restaurants with performing seals. Executive offices with big French windows filled with one-way glass, a trap door to an oubliette below for unpleasant visitors, and a huge picture of Will Rogers "hung conspicuously and intended . . . to suggest" the producer's "essential kinship with Hollywood's St. Francis." Jacques La Borwitz, assistant producer—simply the name! Talent scouts with talking orangoutangs, who have to be told that there aren't any monkeys in Eugene O'Neill's *The Hairy Ape*. Conferences over million dollar picture budgets, when the room grows so silent with expectation you can hear a gray chunk of ash fall from a cigar in midair. Sprawling over a promontory, an unfinished beach house to which some props have been brought for a premature party—"some grass and things." A fallen star with paradisical memories—"thirty acres, with a miniature golf course and a pool and a gorgeous view. All spring I was up to my ass in daisies."

Grotesque fantasy! But it is a grotesque fantasy seen by a writer who knew it well and remained, like Cecilia Brady, "obstinately unhorrified." So the reality comes through, and we recognize the essential America in the fable. It is an America in which "the earth quaked under us" and thirty acres of fairyland tumbled together "like fragments of stories dancing in an open fire." The fault is only superficially geological, just as the crazy fairyland is only partly the thirty-acre back lot of a Hollywood studio following an earthquake. For the earthquake, which occurs early in the novel, is an analogue for the economic depression that wrenched apart American reality and American dream, leaving a gaping fissure between the jumbled remnants. And the last tycoon, a master of illusion sprung from the pragmatic, utilitarian bowels of America, struggles to keep his footing on the slippery pile of rubble while holding aloft the fragments of the binding dream.

But the binding dream is a paradoxical one, even as Stahr is a paradoxical figure. Inspiring Stahr and underlying the montage of chaos that Fitzgerald so brilliantly re-creates as the Hollywood of *The Last Tycoon*, it is at once dream and nightmare. Perhaps "spoiled dream" would be a good way to describe it, suggesting thereby the source of that ambivalent individualist ethic—as Fitzgerald does historically through his symbolic use of the spoils system in the novel—that has been, for good and ill, the making of America.

It is, after all, as merchant of talent—"I want to buy what's in your mind"—that Stahr achieves his status as a heroic individualist. A representative figure of melting-pot America, incorporating the characteristics of shrewd Yankee peddler and wily Jewish merchant raised to the nth degree in the service of a Roman—and American—ideal of practical accomplishment, Stahr is the mythic embodiment of the American dream. Nourished by "health, vitality, ambition, and love," the dream has run its course, like Stahr himself. When the novel opens, his health has failed, his vitality is waning, his love but a ghost. Only ambition, the crude essence of the aspiring individualist, remains. It remains, too, at the heart of the dream, which is, no doubt, why it fails, "consumed with that which it was nourished by."

7

"Begin with an Individual . . ."

"I now get 2,000 a story," Fitzgerald wrote to John Peale Bishop in the spring of 1925, "and they grow worse and worse and my ambition is to get where I need write no more but only novels." Happily he was not to have his wish to be relieved of the necessity of writing short stories, for he still had some good ones to write, although the later stories came in at much lower prices than the two thousand dollars or more he could command for a single story at the peak of his vogue during the twenties as a writer for popular magazines like *The Saturday Evening Post*. As to the quality of the stories, uneven is perhaps the best way to describe them. Like the little girl with the curl in the old rhyme, when Fitzgerald was good he was very, very good and when he was bad he was often horrid.

Fitzgerald regarded himself as, above all, a novelist. The stories were largely means to an end—largely but not entirely, Ernest Hemingway's assertion to the contrary notwithstanding. In A *Moveable Feast,* Hemingway purports to give Fitzgerald's attitude toward his stories in a reported conversation early in their acquaintance in Paris. "He had told me at the Closerie des Lilas how he wrote what he thought were good stories, and which really were good stories for the *Post,"* says Hemingway, "and then changed them for submission, knowing exactly how he must make the twists that made them into salable magazine stories. I had been shocked at this," Hemingway continues, "and I said I thought it was whoring. He said it was whoring but that he had to do it as he made his money from the magazines to have money ahead to write decent books." Of course, Hemingway is making a point about his own literary virtue here and is using Fitzgerald by way of contrast, to illustrate his own rectitude. The point of the story is that Hemingway didn't whore, which is as it may be.

The fact of the matter is, Fitzgerald was a commercially successful short-story writer who, in his palmiest days, earned large sums for a single story. And he thought of that income as necessary to maintain a standard of living—a standard increasingly extravagant during the middle years of his writing career—sufficient to enable him to enjoy life and to devote his most serious efforts to his novels. But he was also a craftsman with high standards and considerable critical insight into the quality of his own work. To be sure, he might fail to live up to his standards from time to time, particularly when he was ill, tired from overwork, or harried for money. Then he did produce trash. But these stories were exceptions, and he was embarrassed by them.

Fitzgerald generally knew when his work was bad. Sending a story to his agent, Harold Ober, he said, "This is one of the lousiest stories I've ever written. Just terrible! . . . Please—and I mean this—don't offer it to the *Post. . . .* Nor to the *Redbook.* It hasn't one redeeming touch of my usual spirit in it." But he did not grow worse and worse as he grew older. On the contrary, some of his later stories, like "Babylon Revisited," are among his best, though he continued to write bad stories—most of the Pat Hobby stories, for example, hardly repay a second reading—along with good ones right to the end.

In other words, commercial success did not necessarily imply poor quality. As a matter of fact, many of his best stories were first published in popular magazines; thus "Babylon Revisited" and "The Ice Palace" originally appeared in *The Saturday Evening Post,* "Winter Dreams" in *Metropolitan Magazine,* "The Rich Boy" in *Redbook,* and "Crazy Sunday" in *American Mercury.* And though he doubtless wrote too many stories, the rapidity with which he turned them out was no index of inadequacy either. In fact, rapidity of execution was one of Fitzgerald's principles as a short-story writer. "Stories are best written in either one jump or three, according to length," he wrote to his daughter when she was at Vassar, nursing ambitions as a writer. "The three-jump story," he explains, "should be done on three successive days, then a day or so for revise and off she goes. This of course is an ideal—"

He didn't always live up to the ideal. Many stories he worked on for months, revising, patching, reconceiving, but frequently such labored efforts were ultimately scrapped. Rarely did they turn out to be among his more creditable stories. On the other hand, the stories completed with the flush of their original conception still upon them often have a freshness and verve, a "bloom" that too much handling might well have dissipated. The Basil and Josephine stories, discussed in an earlier chapter, were so conceived and written. And though they were written when Fitzgerald was in his early thirties, remote from the adolescent years they describe, they were dashed off in the immediacy of recollection and are, most of them, as fresh and lively as the days they summon back.

Actually the springs of Fitzgerald's talent as a writer were various and seemingly contradictory. Though he considered himself primarily a novelist, he recognized that his inspiration was basically poetic. "The talent that matures early is usually of the poetic type, which mine was in large part," he says in reflecting upon his work. In fact, his first concern with literature as a serious art came at Princeton under the tutelage of John Peale Bishop, who taught him to understand and love poetry. The love was lifelong, focussing mainly on the Romantic poets, particularly the Keats of the great odes—"Ode to a Nightingale" and "Ode on a Grecian Urn." They were his touchstones of high art: "Knowing these things very young and granted an ear, one could scarcely ever afterwards be unable to distinguish between gold and dross in what one read." And his advice to Scottie at Vassar included not only specific information about his own technique as a short-story writer but a recommendation that she read Keats and Browning and try writing sonnets. "The only thing that will help you is poetry," he wrote, "which is the most concentrated form of style."

The concentrated expression of deeply felt personal emotional experience lies at the heart of Fitzgerald's work. Commenting in his notebook on the reflection in his work of deeply felt experiences, from his rejection by his first girl, Ginevra King, to his betrayal as a screen writer by producer Joseph Mankiewicz, Fitzgerald says: "taking things hard—from Genevra [sic] to Joe Mank—that's the stamp that goes into my books so that people can read it blind like braille."

For like Keats or like the Byron of *Childe Harold*, Fitzgerald lived in his stories. "I can never remember the times when I write anything," he says in his notebook. *"This Side of Paradise* time or *Beautiful and Damned* or *Gatsby* time, for instance. Lived in story." He is, to be sure, commenting here on the writing of the novels, but the observation applies to the stories as well—at least, to the best of them. It is in fact this quality of intensely experienced emotional life that gives his best work its veracity. Thus his best stories have a quality of reality superior to that of everyday life, more intense, like that of the great Romantic poets. Hence Fitzgerald can speak of sometimes reading his own books for advice and can comment on the differences between what he finds there and his everyday self. "How much I know sometimes—how little at others."

The difference between the daily and the poetical self is, of course, a relative one, and the quantity of knowledge displayed by the latter varies considerably from story to story. For though the insight into reality provided by the poetical self is an emotional, intuitive thing, immediately apprehended, its expression in art requires careful articulation, the subtle work of the master craftsman. And Fitzgerald was often less than masterly. Describing himself in a letter to Maxwell Perkins as "a plodder" who has to "struggle over every point" when he wants to be "serious," Fitzgerald deplores his lack of facility as a writer and admits, "I have a faculty for being cheap, if I wanted to indulge that. I can do cheap things."

Indeed he could, and often did. And, in fact, his very conception of what is serious is often flawed, his valid emotional insights vitiated or obscured by cheap claptrappery. As to his lack of facility, one sometimes wishes that he had less of it and that he had struggled harder over many of his points.

The gap between perception and execution is well illustrated in an early story, "The Diamond as Big as the Ritz," based on the experience of a summer vacation following Fitzgerald's sophomore year at college, when he stayed at the Donahoe ranch near White Sulpher Springs, Montana, with his Princeton friend Sap Donahoe. The ranch was remote and isolate under the big sky of Montana. Vistas were tremendous, dwarfing human significance, especially so for a boy from the Midwest who had spent most of his recent years at school and college in the East. Moreover, Sap's family was wealthy, and their ranch was large; it must have seemed enormous to a young man who had lived on the fringe of St. Paul's upper middle class and who had known himself to be, a couple of years earlier at prep school, the poorest boy in a rich boys' school. Fascinated by great wealth, Fitzgerald was later to write he cherished "an abiding distrust, an animosity, toward the leisure class—not the conviction of a revolutionist but the smouldering hatred of a peasant." That hatred was to be ignited by an event that followed shortly after his visit to the Donahoe ranch; namely, his dismissal as a suitor by the wealthy Ginevra King. She had won his heart. Shortly she was to reject him for a more suitably wealthy mate, leaving a permanent scar on Fitzgerald's psyche.

The awesomeness of nature and the potential power of vast wealth, indifferent alike to the plight of man, conjoin as threats under the impact of a deeply felt emotional experience for Fitzgerald and are reflected in "The Diamond as Big as the Ritz." The very atmosphere is malevolent in a landscape where "the Montana sunset lay between two mountains like a gigantic bruise from which dark arteries spread themselves over a poisoned sky." In that atmosphere "crouched the village of Fish, minute, dismal, and forgotten." The twelve men of the village, "sombre and inexplicable souls," are "a race apart . . . like some species developed by an early whim of nature. . . ." They sustain a relationship with the rest of mankind only through the thin thread of the railroad, in token of which they might have deified, in this God-forsaken world, "the Great Brakeman."

The threatening, macabre atmosphere created in the opening pages of "The Diamond as Big as the Ritz" is appropriate to the definition of human evil consequent upon the possession of great wealth that lies at the heart of the story. The wealth is the Braddock Washingtons', embodied in a gigantic diamond underlying their ranch, which John Unger, the central character in the story, visits with his schoolmate Percy Washington during summer vacation. There John discovers the evil, too, when he learns that he like former victims will be put to death at the end of his visit to protect the secret of the Washington fortune. That evil is pervasive, corrupting even the young and innocent. Thus Kismine, Percy's sister, selfishly accepts the human sacrifices her father demands in order to insure the secret of the great diamond on which the Washington fortune is based. "We can't let such an inevitable thing as death stand in the way of enjoying life while we have it," she rationalizes. "Think how lonesome it'd be out here if we never had *any*one. Why father and mother have sacrificed some of their best friends just as we have."

Some of our best friends—have gone to the gas chambers!

To be sure, such ugly facts are not to be dwelt upon.

When young John Unger, who has fallen in love with Kismine, learns that house guests are liquidated at the end of the summer—"It's only natural for us to get all the pleasure out of them that we can first," she coolly affirms—he protests that she has been kissing a corpse. " 'You're not a corpse!' she protested in horror. 'You're not a corpse! I won't have you saying that I kissed a corpse.' "

Insulated by wealth, Kismine's very innocence is an expression of the corrupting influence of money. When John Unger tells her of the complaints of another rich girl who has but four maids to help her, Kismine responds: "It's absurd. . . . Think of all the millions and millions of people in the world, laborers and all, who get along with only two maids." And when the black slaves are killed in a bombing raid on the Washington compound at the end of the story, her response is "There go fifty thousand dollars' worth of slaves . . . at prewar prices. So few Americans have any respect for property."

Respect for property! Her indignation anticipates the middle-class response to race riots, occasioned by the repression of blacks, and the use of the phrase "law and order" as code words for the toleration of de facto segregation. In fact the story perceptively exposes American racial stereotypes and prejudices. When Mr. Braddock Washington mentions the "period of absurd idealism" of his youth, when he equipped every slave's room with a tile bath, John Unger responds: "I suppose . . . that they used the bath tubs to keep coal in." Mr. Washington interrupts him "coldly" to say: "My slaves did not keep coal in their bathtubs. . . . I discontinued the baths for quite another reason. Several of them caught cold and died. Water is not good for certain races—except as a beverage."

Actually the very name Washington and the tracing of

the family history back to the Father of Our Country is an indictment of the exploitative nature of American society under the domination of laissez-faire capitalism. Perhaps it was the impulse underlying this story that Fitzgerald had in mind when, jotting in his notebook an enigmatic and rather misleading comparison between himself and D. H. Lawrence, he characterized the latter as "essentially pre-Marxian," and added, "Just as I am essentially Marxian."

The conclusion of the story, however, is far from Marxian—and far from satisfactory. When the Washington redoubt is destroyed and all the family with it, except for Kismine and her sister who escape with John Unger, penniless, into the world, John ends the story on an inflated rhetorical note of sentimental pessimism. "Let us love for a while, for a year or so, you and me," he says to Kismine. "That's a form of divine drunkenness that we can all try. There are only diamonds in the whole world, diamonds and perhaps the shabby gift of disillusion. Well, I have that last and I will make the usual nothing of it." We know, of course, that there are more things than diamonds and disillusion even in John Unger's world, and we suspect that Fitzgerald knows and that he has made the reduction to alliterate with divine drunkenness rather than to coincide with the truth.

But there is much else that is unsatisfactory in "The Diamond as Big as the Ritz." There is for example the beginning, in Hades, which is productive of a bad joke and indicative of Fitzgerald's uncertainty in the handling of fantasy, for he cannot decide whether his conception is allegorical or symbolic. The result is neither; it is simply tiresome.

Tiresome, too, is the business of the automobile—immense, bejeweled, and so forth—that transports Unger and his schoolmate host to the Washingtons' pasticcio Shangri-la. And, of course, the impedimenta of that mountain-top hideaway are too lengthily dwelt upon. Fitzgerald sidetracks the evil power of his story for long stretches of schoolboy luxuriance in bathtub rainbows of pink foam, peacock soup, sable-covered floors, golf courses that are all green, and similar nonsense.

Worst of all, the very victims of that inhuman wealth, which is made so potent a force of evil in the story, are depicted as mere clowns. The adventurers who have stumbled on Braddock Washington's El Dorado and are imprisoned in a silly fishbowl prison sunk into the golf course lack all dignity. Ludicrously Fitzgerald has them make stupid jokes, sing songs and rage, when they do so, with the feeble execrations of comic-strip figures.

Thus "The Diamond as Big as the Ritz" is a story that one reads with interest for its powerful depiction of the dreadful implications of vast wealth, but with increasing irritation at Fitzgerald's betrayal of that central theme, which he trivializes.

"The Ice Palace," on the other hand, is another story altogether. Though it, too, is a relatively early one it reveals a surer hand than is evident in "The Diamond as Big as the Ritz." Beginning and ending in a sleepy Southern town bathed in languorous sunshine and nourishing warm human relationships and happily sentimental attitudes toward the still-living ghosts of its dead past, it is the story of Sally Carrol Happer, an intermittently restless beauty who goes North to marry. But she doesn't stay. She returns to the warm human tolerance and kindly patience of Tarleton, Georgia, from the busy rigor and puritanical chill of the Northern city where she has visited her energetic boor of a fiancé.

The story's meaning is implicit in the contrast of images of warmth and iciness associated with Tarleton and the nameless Northern city that Sally Carrol visits. The images grow naturally from the story, culminating in a symbolic ice palace, the central feature of a winter carnival that Harry Bellamy, the Northern beau, takes her to. And she gets lost in the caves of ice—her allusion to Coleridge's "Kubla Khan" reinforces the symbolic meaning—of the carnival's glacial alternative to a pleasure dome. Exhausted and hysterical, she is finally rescued by Roger Patton, a free spirit whose intellectual concerns have kept him unfrozen in this blood-congealing Northern milieu.

At one point in the story Sally Carrol tells Roger why she will marry Bellamy. "I'm the sort of person who wants to be taken care of after a certain point," she says, "and I feel sure I will be." There is a nice ambiguity in that "after a certain point." After a certain point, life gives way to the frozen security of death. We may be sure that with Harry Bellamy she would have been taken care of, incarcerated in the ice palace, a perfect symbol for the rigid portentousness of a people "righteous, narrow, and cheerless, without infinite possibilities for great sorrow or joy."

Happily a token incarceration is sufficient. And Sally Carrol returns from the caves of ice to sunny Tarleton, there to be fed not, to be sure, on paradisical honey-dew but on Georgia's promising April equivalent—green peaches.

But April's promise is not often fulfilled.

> April is the cruellest month, breeding
> Lilacs out of the dead land, mixing
> Memory with desire, stirring
> Dull roots with spring rain.

T. S. Eliot's lines from "The Waste Land" might serve as an epigraph for Fitzgerald's "Winter Dreams," published in

1922, the same year as Eliot's poem. Ironically reversing traditional expectations of fruition in the fullness of the burgeoning year, both poem and story are concerned with the failure of that promise, a failure attributable to the drying up of the inner springs of life. Both works grow out of profoundly disturbing personal experiences, in Fitzgerald's case the loss of rich, beautiful Ginevra King. This led, for Fitzgerald, to a qualification of his belief that he could always get the "top girl," who represented success for him, possession of the "glittering things" of life. The consequences were two: either the ideal was faulty or the seeker was flawed. In the former instance, the top girl turns out to be a bitch goddess, luring men who serve her to their destruction, as for example, Daisy Buchanan does in *The Great Gatsby*. In the latter case, the author's surrogate finds *himself* lacking, an emotional bankrupt who gives out before the goal is obtained, or arriving at the anticipated goal he discovers that it has lost its ability to satisfy. The classic illustration is Dick Diver in *Tender Is the Night*. And this latter pattern is generally thought to be the consequence of the experience in Fitzgerald's life that led to his self-styled crack-up. However, one can see the pattern anticipated in Dexter Green of "Winter Dreams," a story written twelve years before *Tender Is the Night*.

That story for all its surface glitter is an exceptionally bleak one. Beginning with Dexter's recognition that "there was something dismal about this Northern spring" and that the grandiose dreams of winter melt and run away to nothing, the story progresses through a series of negations. Dexter's first discovery, for example, is the discovery that, at fourteen, he is already "too old." It is followed by his decision, at the very beginning of the story, "to quit." To be sure, these are childish discoveries and decisions, humorous, in the way the Basil stories sometimes are, in their adolescent parody of adult roles. But this is not a Basil story, where youthful experience is carefully framed and set off as nostalgic recollection. Here youth flows into maturity. Dexter's response is occasioned by his awakening to awareness of the complexities of adult life in the precocious femininity of eleven-year-old Judy Jones, who imperiously demands that he caddy for her, a demand which he responds to by quitting his job as a caddy so overbearing is she.

Of course, Dexter's renunciation of the world that he sees Judy dominating leads to success in business and his conquest of the adult world, since he forgoes pleasure to concentrate on getting ahead. But even at the beginning of that conquest, the victory turns sour. Admitted to membership at the fashionable golf course where he had caddied as a boy, he discovers that Mr. T. A. Hedrick, who represents the values toward which he aspires, is "a bore and not even a good golfer any more."

Then there is Judy Jones herself, whom Dexter later wins. But he holds her for a brief moment only. "There was a fish jumping and a star shining and the lights around the lake were gleaming." The repetition of that refrain beautifully marks the limits of that suspended moment in their romantic love. Romantic love, as we know, lives in the suspended moment. Its emblem is the dream, not the altar or the marriage bed. But the dream sustains the ecstasy in the romantic tradition. Commenting on Dexter's love for Judy, Fitzgerald says at one point in the story, "There was all the ecstasy of an engagement about it, sharpened by his realization that there was no engagement." That is the essence of romantic love. Since he does not possess her, "she cannot fade." But Judy does fade—fades into marriage and respectability and children and the ignominy of a philandering husband. That is no part of the romantic ideal.

In point of fact, we might have anticipated such a dénouement, for Fitzgerald presents Dexter's idol as a puppet, "a slender enamelled doll in cloth of gold." Behind the enamelled facade is only a Judy, not a Laura, an Isabel, a Maria, or a Ginevra; just Judy Jones, who belongs next door with an unfaithful husband and a swarm of kids.

Actually, Judy, with her cloth of gold dress, "gold in a band at her head, gold in two slipper points at her dress's hem" is but one manifestation of those "glittering things and glittering people" that Dexter wanted. The other is his business career, in which he makes a success, winning great wealth. In the concluding section of the story, Fitzgerald says, "This story is not his biography, remember, although things creep into it which have nothing to do with those dreams he had when he was young." He is speaking presumably of Dexter's doing so well in New York "that there were no barriers too high for him." And, in a way, that is true. His success in business has been, in one sense, a consequence of his quitting the golf course as a boy, of his turning away from the sphere that Judy dominates at the center of the story. He rises by refusing to accept domination either by the life of pleasure or by those who have access to it. It is accomplished with the "hard-minded" part of him that operates in the interstices of his preoccupation with Judy, offhandedly almost. But the two elements of the story are inextricably bound together, and things creep in which appear to have nothing to do with others, but do. Even in turning away from the golf course, Dexter makes his success by washing, in his laundries, the golfing stockings and sweaters of the men who play and the lingerie of their women. Even in feeling himself younger and stronger than the men of leisure and grace at college, he wishes his children to be like them and sees himself as "the rough, strong stuff from which they eternally sprang." Even as a nobody whose father owned the second-best grocery store in a fashionable resort, Dexter, in turning away from Judy, creates the future that makes association with her possible.

What the story turns out to be about is thus not the loss of romantic love. Bleaker than that, it is about the impossibility of love. For the glittering beloved is, in a sense, compounded of the very stuff one would sacrifice to achieve her: dominance, power, the wealth and worldly success that romantic love is an alternative to. Winning what he needs to win her—dominion, power, dollars—he has the substance that she symbolizes and no longer needs her. Her inhumanity is matched—ultimately—by his own. The bitterest fact of the story is not Dexter's loss of the girl. It is his loss of his dream. Dexter's tears at the end of "Winter Dreams" are not for Judy; they are for his lost self.

"Winter Dreams" ends on a plangent note, with Dexter Green's recognition that "long ago, there was something in me, but now that thing is gone." The plangency and the rhetoric are absent in "The Rich Boy," the story of Anson Hunter, who also loves and loses. Partly the absence can be explained by Fitzgerald's strict control of point of view. "Let me tell you about the very rich. They are different from you and me." So says the nameless narrator. And he continues, "The only way I can describe Anson Hunter is to approach him as if he were a foreigner and cling stubbornly to my point of view. If I accept his for a moment I am lost—I have nothing to show but a preposterous movie."

Preposterous movie indeed! Anson Hunter's conception of himself is determined by his role as rich boy to such a degree that he has no proper self. "Begin with an individual," Fitzgerald says in the opening sentence of the story, "and before you know it you find that you have created a type. . . ." The story of Anson Hunter is the story of an individual hollowed out by the corrosive effects of extreme wealth until nothing remains but the type. He is the rich boy who sacrifices others—Paula, Dolly, Edna, Cary Sloane —to the image of his own power, importance, centrality. In doing so, he loses passion, affection, friendship—everything, emptying himself in obedience to the demand of a role. The story, a fine one, is a dramatically understated revelation of this reductive process.

In a poetic "April Letter" that Fitzgerald wrote in 1935, when he was going through one of his most serious emotional crises, he says: "I have asked a lot of my emotions—one hundred and twenty stories. The price was high, right up with Kipling, because there was one little drop of something—not blood, not a tear, not my seed, but me more intimately than these, in every story, it was the extra I had." And since he felt himself at a turning point in his career, worked out and emotionally bankrupt, he concludes, "Now it has gone and I am just like you now."

Fitzgerald was right, in a sense. He had in fact reached a turning point in his career in 1935. But he was not just like anyone else. He still had something "extra" that was to provide the basis for the final phase of his career. It was another quality that he shared with Keats, the Keats who lived projectively—beyond himself. This was the Keats who in describing the poetical character observed, "It lives in gusto be it foul or fair, high or low, rich or poor, mean or elevated," and who upon seeing a sparrow before his window said, "I take part in its existence and pick about the gravel."

"When I like men," Fitzgerald observed in his notebook, "I want to be like them—I want to lose the outer qualities that give me my individuality and be like them. I don't want the man; I want to absorb into myself all the qualities that make him attractive and leave him out. I cling to my own innards."

Clinging to one's own innards while living dramatically in the outer qualities of other men is a difficult task, one that has been achieved by few artists except the great dramatic poets. Neither Keats nor Fitzgerald quite reached that goal, though both aspired to it toward the close of their lives. Perhaps Fitzgerald's closest approximation was in *The Last Tycoon*, which he was struggling to finish when he died.

In that unfinished book and in several stories of his last years, Fitzgerald leaves behind the torturing uncertainty of *Tender Is the Night*, which explored introspectively what he thought to be his own emotional bankruptcy. "I have now become a writer only," he said in "Pasting It Together." He had not, in fact, become "a writer only" in the reductive sense he implied in that essay. But the best of his later work has an objective dramatic quality. His prose is spare; he is less apt to indulge in metaphor and fancy diction than he once did. Nostalgia disappears. His tone is cool, avoiding rhetorical embellishment.

"Babylon Revisited," though it was written as early as 1931, is a story of this sort. Told with great economy, it is a story of waste—waste of time, money, life, love, everything. One sees this first through the eyes of Charlie Wales, who has returned to Paris, scene of his former dissipation, to recover custody of his daughter. And there, amidst his old haunts, he comes to a realization of the utter triviality of his former life. "All the catering to vice and waste," he sees on revisiting a Montmartre night spot, "was on an utterly childish scale, and he suddenly realized the meaning of the word "dissipate"—to dissipate into thin air; to make nothing out of something."

The insight is given dramatic point by virtue of the contrast of that life with the new life possible to Charlie and his nine-year-old daughter Honoria, whose simple warmth and charm makes "childish" seem a totally inadequate term to apply to the senseless and malicious behavior of a pair of ghosts who turn up from Charlie's reveling past. These ghosts are Duncan Schaeffer and Lorraine Quarrles, and their presence not only threatens Charlie's new life, it brings the viciousness of his old one horribly alive. For their intrusion into the domestic milieu of the Peters, Honoria's legal custodians, on the night her return to her father is to be decided is as destructive of that future as Charlie's locking his wife out in the snow in drunken anger had been destructive of her. That had been back in twenty-nine at the height of the wasteful binge when, as Charlie recalls, "the snow . . . wasn't real snow. If you didn't want it to be snow, you just paid some money."

Ironically Charlie just keeps on paying. For the story ends with Charlie forced to substitute sending Honoria "a lot of things tomorrow" for the future with its affectionate relationship of a father and daughter living happily together that seemed probable. The irony is double. Charlie has withstood the temptation of another plunge into Babylon. The plunge hasn't even been a temptation. He has been defeated this time by the hatred of Marion Peters, whose terrible bitterness is another indirect consequence of the wasted years in Charlie's life. Charlie has tried to recoup those years, to make something out of his life. He is not able to because Marion's arrogant virtue stands in his way. She has known him to be a wastrel; now she will make certain that the waste is complete, that he will not enjoy the domestic happiness that she sees as her exclusive right. And arrogant virtue has power, like self-indulgent vice, "to dissipate into thin air; to make nothing out of something."

Fitzgerald certainly had enough experience of waste of all kinds, most of it sufficiently close to the events of the story to make this a luxuriantly sentimental remembrance of things past. But the story is nothing of the sort. Its great virtue is its economy. There is no room for lamentation, nor is there ultimately any need for it. Charlie, though defeated in his effort to make a new life with his daughter, acquits himself well in his second temptation, resisting drink and false friends and rising above both anger at unjust or excessive penalties for his former frailties and emotional self-indulgence in their recall.

> Nothing is here, for tears, nothing to wail
> Or knock the breast, no weakness, no contempt,
> Dispraise or blame, nothing but well and fair.

Charlie acquits himself—as Fitzgerald did—accepting his due measure of responsibility for a wasted past, but triumphing over it in his effort to make the best of however limited a present remains. One might say the emotion is in the economy in this spare story of waste.

"Crazy Sunday" is another story of self-indulgence manifested, lamented, and placed in a broader context that modifies our initial response to the Fitzgerald-like character who is its protagonist. A complex story, it begins with Joel Coles, a Hollywood writer who finds release from the pressures of his job on what he calls Crazy Sunday, when he turns to drink and exhibitionism after a week of restraint, making a fool of himself. On Monday he laments the damage done to his self-esteem, his career prospects, and the people he has demeaned through his behavior. It has all the elements of a self-pitying study of Fitzgerald's career in Hollywood.

But the center of interest quickly shifts from Joel to Miles Calman, a film director of genius and an early version of Stahr, the hero of *The Last Tycoon*. Miles' self-indulgence is Eva Goebel, whom his wife Stella has found out about. And Stella's self-indulgence is Joel, whom she attempts to seduce in revenge for Miles' betrayal. But Miles is killed in an airplane crash while the seduction is in progress, and her attempt to complete the seduction is really an effort to keep Calman alive. As Joel thinks incredulously when he reflects on the episode, "Stella was trying to keep Miles alive by sustaining a situation in which he had figured—as if Miles' mind could not die so long as the possibilities that had worried him still existed."

Joel resists the temptation to give Miles a life after death and goes home, realizing as he does so that Stella Calman is a mere puppet. A creation of Miles, she is trying to make Joel into an imitation of her husband. Her very taste in men, himself included, is but a reflection of Miles' admiration. "Everything he touched he did something magical to," Joel reflects. "He even brought that little gamin alive and made her a sort of masterpiece."

The sort of masterpiece she is, is in the completeness of her gamin quality, the waif so totally "taken up" that she takes up Joel as an extension of Miles. But the magical hand of the master works beyond that rather grotesquely limited end. Godlike—this is "crazy" Sunday—Miles is alive in Joel, whom he has formed, too. Joel's refusal to stay the night and "comfort" Stella is a reflection of the degree to which he is no mere imitation of Miles but, in his own way, the real thing.

The real thing—that was what Fitzgerald was after to

the very end. And toward the end—indeed from the thirties on—he turns from his own intensely recalled past to find it in the very world about him. Often in stories like "Babylon Revisited," "Crazy Sunday," and others, he makes of any little gamin or reformed drunk or Hollywood director "a sort of masterpiece"; that is to say, eliminating himself, he makes of them the fullest expression of their imagined potential.

8

The Garden of Allah

Someone once told Sheilah Graham that she had wonderful teeth, and from the photographic evidence in her autobiography, *Beloved Infidel*, it would seem that she never shut her mouth thereafter but always wore the inane grin of the girl in the toothpaste ads. One wonders how the gray-faced ghost who lived in—of all places—the Garden of Allah apartments with her could have borne such persistent cheeriness. And how did he withstand the puerility of Sheilah Graham's gossip column "Hollywood Today"? Perhaps part of her appeal was that, for all her strength of will, she was obviously completely without talent, and he never had to fear her as a rival, as he feared, however needlessly, Zelda. Happily Fitzgerald didn't live to read Miss Graham's book. Imagine the response of the master ironist to this inane bit, as his mistress reflects on the adieu of her prospective husband, the Marquis of Donegall: " 'Goodby, your ladyship,' he said, and kissed me. I drove back lost in lovely dreams. *Your ladyship!*"

As it transpired, Miss Graham didn't marry the Marquis of Donegall but threw him over to live with Fitzgerald, sacrificing thereby the London waif's dream of gentility for the Hollywood gossip columnist's dream of literary respectability. All things considered, the sacrifice was not so great, earls being in relatively cheap supply as compared to writers of genius. It was not until after the relationship was well established that real sacrifices were required, for the writer of genius was also an alcoholic who maliciously tried to destroy Sheilah's career, such as it was, threatened her life, almost took his own, and periodically spent days "drying out" under medical supervision.

One such debauch took Fitzgerald clear across the country, from Hollywood to Hanover, New Hampshire, where a motion-picture cast was assembled on location, filming a script based on the Dartmouth Winter Carnival that he and the young writer Budd Schulberg were scheduled to complete. The two writers flew East with Sheilah Graham and a magnum of champagne, which started Fitzgerald off. He was tiddly in New York, where they dropped Sheilah, sloshed on the train to Hanover, and roaring drunk for most of the week that he and Schulberg spent in Hanover, where Fitzgerald was by turns truculent, maudlin, silly, and comatose. Finally, Walter Wanger, the producer who had assigned the pair to the film and watched their distressing antics at Dartmouth, fired both of them and ordered them to leave town. Fitzgerald ended up in the Doctors' Hospital in New York City. It was two weeks before Miss Graham was able to escort the shaky ashen wreck back to Hollywood.

Such outbreaks were sporadic, set off by any one of a number of apparently trivial events that triggered the mechanism of self-loathing and desire for obliteration in a sick, exhausted man. The desire surfaces in a letter to Sheilah Graham, written after a violent, drunken physical assault on her. "I'm glad you no longer can think of me with either respect or affection," Fitzgerald comments, "I'm *horrible* for you." And noting that "something was terribly wrong" with their relationship, he concludes, "I was it. Not fit for any human relation. . . . I want to die, Sheilah, and in my own way."

Doubtless the persistent drinking was an expression of Fitzgerald's death wish. But just as the moralist was intertwined with the hedonist in Fitzgerald, so the death wish was coupled with a tenacious will to live and to wring from life, in the face of defeats and disappointments, all that it could offer. Hollywood was an escape after the apparent failure of *Tender Is the Night* and the emotional bankruptcy depicted in *The Crack-Up*. But it was also a challenge. Fitzgerald wanted to master the new medium of film, and he worked hard at it, only to have his best efforts spoiled, more often than not, by the blundering efforts of a producer whose only interests were commercial ones. His response to such interference is indicated in his letter to Joe Mankiewicz, the producer who botched his work on the film version of *Three Comrades*. "To say I'm disillusioned," he says in his letter to Mankiewicz, "is putting it mildly. . . . I feel . . . outraged." His attitude is not that of the untouchable artist but of the responsible craftsman who knows his business and sees his work being bungled by awkward hands. "For nineteen years," his letter states, "I've written best selling entertainment, and my dialogue is supposedly right up at the top. But I learn from the script that you've suddenly decided that it isn't good dialogue and you can take a few hours off and do much better." And he concludes, "Oh, Joe, can't producers ever be wrong? I'm a good writer—honest. I thought you were going to play fair. Joan Crawford might as well play the part now, for the thing is as groggy with sentimentality as *The Bride Wore Red*, but the true emotion is gone."

Fitzgerald didn't get fair treatment in Hollywood, but he persisted nonetheless, doing longer or shorter writing stints on *Infidelity*—renamed *Fidelity* because of trouble with the censors—*The Barretts of Wimpole Street*, *The Women, Madame Curie, Gone With the Wind*, and *The Light of Heart*, among other scripts, working on a picture until the whims governing an irrational production system dictated his removal. Ironically, this sort of work earned him $88,391 during his first eighteen months in Hollywood, enabling him to pay off most of his debts, put his insurance policies, against which he had borrowed heavily, in order, and keep his daughter Scottie at Vassar. This latter expense was no small one. Fitzgerald's letters to his daughter are filled with references to debts paid and money sent for a variety of needs. One of his letters to her ends with the dourly humorous postcript: "Have paid Peck & Peck & Peck & Peck & Peck."

Irony lies in the fact that Fitzgerald's real potential as a film writer, if indeed he had any, was ignored and wasted. His fine short story "Babylon Revisited" had been sold to Lester Cowan, the producer, for a relatively small sum. Fitzgerald was given a minimal fee, by Hollywood standards, for adapting it to the screen. But the picture was not produced. After Fitzgerald's death, Cowan took the script Fitzgerald had fashioned off the shelf and asked another writer to revise it. The writer's response upon examining it was: "This is the most perfect motion-picture scenario I have ever read. I don't see why you want to revise it." And Cowan is reported to have said, "You're absolutely right. I'll pay you two thousand dollars a week to stay out here and keep me from changing one word of it." Hollywood! The episode might have come from *The Last Tycoon*.

To be sure, there is another side to the story. It is difficult to see how anyone could describe "Cosmopolitan," the scenario Fitzgerald made from "Babylon Revisited," as a perfect script. Expanded with extraneous detail to make it into a full-length film, it is cluttered with a gangster subplot and a sentimental love story between Charles Wales and a nurse. The result is that the center of the original story—the relationship between Charles and his daughter —is submerged beneath the kind of shoddy sensationalism that Stahr complains about to Boxley in *The Last Tycoon*. Working with his own original material, Fitzgerald only succeeds in cheapening and confusing what had been clear and beautiful. Perhaps his talent was not especially suited to the movies. A letter written about this time to his old friend Kate Tighe seems to confess as much: "The movies went to my head, and I tried to lick the set up single-handed and came out a sadder and wiser man."

"Isn't Hollywood a dump—in the human sense of the word?" Fitzgerald asks in another letter of 1940. And in yet another—to Gerald Murphy—he refers to it as Armageddon. However, he says, "the new Armageddon, far from making everything unimportant, gives me a certain rebirth of kinetic impulses. . . ." World War II had begun. Fitzgerald was ill and had been confined to bed for over four months. He had had no picture work for a long time. But he was writing fiction again and finding that "after twenty months of moving-pictures it was fun to be back at prose writing again." Indeed with his "great dreams about [Hollywood] shattered," he had started work on *The Last Tycoon* and found that "in the land of the living again I function rather well."

In fact, throughout portions of his last year in Hollywood Fitzgerald hints at a profound change in himself. "I find, after a long time out here," he says in one letter, "that one develops new attitudes." In another, looking back to the painful period of his breakdown he says that "in retrospect it seems . . . a spiritual 'change of life.' " And he goes on to comment on his gradual transformation: "The sensitive cannot make themselves overnight into specimens of the 'tough-minded'—the great ally is time. . . . Time was my rescuer." In yet another letter he speaks "of a new phase, or rather a development of something that began long ago in my writing—to try to dig up the relevant, the essential, and especially the dramatic and glamorous from whatever life is around."

There is, seemingly, little enough of it in Hollywood, this "slack soft place" where "withdrawal is practically a condition of safety," where the "sin is to upset anyone else," and "everywhere there is . . . either corruption or indifference." But whatever there is, he will turn to it as his subject, abandoning the romantic world of his early stories and the nostalgia with which he later looked back upon that world. As for the inner life, there would be no insistent dwelling upon that, as there had been in *Tender Is the Night*, with its probing self-analysis. Instead he would be content to "emphatically cherish what little is left."

Cherishing that bit, he managed to give up drinking. According to Sheilah Graham, he did not have a drink during the last year of his life. Living quietly with Miss Graham at Encino and later in Hollywood, he devoted himself to broadening her mind—he confesses in a letter to having "rather despised her intellectually"—and to his writing. He worked hard at the latter, often writing in bed on an improvised lap desk all day, or as long as his diminished strength held out. He was pleased with the way *The Last Tycoon* was going. "I think my novel is good," he wrote in his last letter to Edmund Wilson. And he recognized that both the novel and the stories he was writing for Arnold Gingrich's *Esquire* and Kenneth Littauer, at *Collier's*, had taken a new direction. "Here's another Hollywood story," he says to Littauer of one of these. "It is absolutely true to Hollywood as I see it." Explaining the difference between his early illusion-filled work and his work since "Babylon Revisited," which signalized the death of these illusions, Fitzgerald concluded, "So you see I've made a sort of turn."

Indeed he had. But he had a short distance to go on the new road. In November 1940 he suffered a cardiac spasm. However, he continued to work on the new book. On December 20 he had a severe heart attack. Then on December 21 as he waited after lunch with Miss Graham in her Laurel Avenue apartment for the doctor to come and take a cardiogram, he had another spasm. Before the doctor arrived, he was dead. He was forty-four years old.

Fitzgerald's fifth novel would never be completed. He had, however, published four others and over 160 stories during his lifetime. Nine of his books were in print. But his reputation had reached its nadir. There was no call for his books. He was not read. In fact, when Budd Schulberg, fresh from Dartmouth, had first been introduced to Fitzgerald in Hollywood, he was taken aback. He had thought that Fitzgerald was dead. Now he was in fact dead—reputation and man together. And the obituaries were content, for the most part, to shovel on dirt, burying both in the grave of the scandalous twenties, the Jazz Age, of which Fitzgerald was superficially taken to be the embodiment and the chronicler.

He was considerably more than that, as Stephen Vincent Benét was to point out the next year, when Edmund Wilson published the fragment of *The Last Tycoon* that Fitzgerald had finished prior to his death, along with Fitzgerald's notes on the novel and a synopsis of the unfinished portion of it. In an article in the *Saturday Review of Literature* that celebrated Fitzgerald's achievement and anticipated his ultimate high place among the ranks of American writers, Benét said in conclusion: ". . . the evidence is in. You can take off your hats now, gentlemen, and I think perhaps you had better. This is not a legend, this is a reputation—and, seen in perspective, it may well be one of the most secure reputations of our time."

Subsequent history has but confirmed that estimate.

A Selected
Bibliography

By Fitzgerald

(DATES REPRESENT FIRST PUBLICATION IN BOOK FORM.)

1920 *This Side of Paradise*
1920 *Flappers and Philosophers*
1922 *The Beautiful and Damned*
1922 *Tales of the Jazz Age*   (STORIES)
1923 *The Vegetable, or From President to Postman* (PLAY)
1925 *The Great Gatsby*
1926 *All the Sad Young Men* (STORIES)
1934 *Tender Is the Night*
1935 *Taps at Reveille* (STORIES)

POSTHUMOUS PUBLICATION

1941 *The Last Tycoon* (unfinished), edited by Edmund Wilson
1945 *The Crack-Up*, edited by Edmund Wilson
1957 *Afternoon of an Author: A Selection of Uncollected*

Stories and Essays with an Introduction and Notes by Arthur Mizener

1963 The Letters of F. Scott Fitzgerald, edited by Andrew Turnbull

1971 Dear Scott-Dear Max: The Fitzgerald-Perkins Correspondence, edited by John Kuehl and Jackson Bryer

By Zelda Sayre Fitzgerald

1932 Save Me the Waltz

About Scott and Zelda Fitzgerald, His Works, and Their Time

Bruccoli, Matthew. The Composition of "Tender Is The Night." Pittsburgh: University of Pittsburgh Press, 1963.

Callaghan, Morley. That Summer in Paris: Memories of Tangled Friendships with Hemingway, Fitzgerald, and Some Others. New York: Coward-McCann, 1963.

Cowley, Malcolm. Exile's Return. New York: Viking Press, 1951.

————, ed. After The Genteel Tradition. Revised Edition. Carbondale, Ill.: University of S. Illinois Press, 1964.

Graham, Sheilah, and Frank, Gerold. Beloved Infidel: The Education of a Woman. New York: Henry Holt & Co., 1958.

Hemingway, Ernest. A Moveable Feast. New York: Charles Scribner's Sons, 1964.

Hindus, Milton. Fitzgerald: An Introduction and Interpretation. New York: Holt, Rinehart and Winston, 1968.

Hoffman, Frederick J. "The Great Gatsby": A Study. New York: Charles Scribner's Sons, 1962.

Kazin, Alfred, ed. F. Scott Fitzgerald: The Man and His Work. New York: World Publishing Co., 1951.

Latham, Aaron. Crazy Sundays. New York: Viking Press, 1972.

Milford, Nancy. Zelda: A Biography. New York: Harper & Row, 1970.

Mizener, Arthur. *The Far Side of Paradise*. Revised Edition. Boston: Houghton Mifflin Co., 1965.

————, ed. *F. Scott Fitzgerald: A Collection of Critical Essays*. Englewood Cliffs, N.J.: Prentice Hall, 1963.

Perkins, Maxwell E. *Editor to Author: The Letters of Maxwell E. Perkins*, edited by John Hall Wheelock. New York: Charles Scribner's Sons, 1950.

Piper, Henry Dan. *F. Scott Fitzgerald: A Critical Portrait*. New York: Holt, Rinehart and Winston, 1965.

Sklar, Robert E. *F. Scott Fitzgerald: The Last Laocoön*. New York: Oxford University Press, 1967.

Stern, Milton R. *The Golden Moment: The Novels of F. Scott Fitzgerald*. Urbana, Ill.: University of Illinois Press, 1970.

Tomkins, Calvin. *Living Well Is the Best Revenge*. New York: Viking Press, 1971.

Turnbull, Andrew. *Scott Fitzgerald*. New York: Charles Scribner's Sons, 1962.

Index

About the Author

William A. Fahey is professor of English at C. W. Post College, Long Island University, Greenvale, New York, where he teaches courses in modern poetry and modern fiction and serves as chairman of the English Department. He received his B.A. from Queens College and his Ph.D. from New York University. He has published articles on James Joyce, D. H. Lawrence, Wallace Stevens, and Flannery O'Connor, among other writers, and has contributed to three books for young people: *Famous American Authors, Our Foreign-Born Citizens,* and *Great American Negroes.*

Dr. Fahey enjoys German lieder, French wine, Oriental rugs, Shaker furniture, and fine prints. He is an organic gardener, a fair carpenter, a poor sailor, and an unrecognized genius at sculpture, having completed one work, in clay. On a forthcoming sabbatical he plans to visit Ireland for research on a book about W. B. Yeats.

He lives in Northport, New York, with his wife Joan, who is a painter, and three children, Jed, Seth, and Toby.